Voices *of*
PRINCES
RISBOROUGH

VOICES *of* PRINCES RISBOROUGH

MIKE AND ANGELA PAYNE

The
History
Press

First published 2009

The History Press
The Mill, Brimscombe Port
Stroud, Gloucestershire, GL5 2QG
www.thehistorypress.co.uk

British Library Cataloguing in Publication Data.
A catalogue record for this book is available from the British Library.

ISBN 978 0 7524 5151 0

Typesetting and origination by The History Press
Printed in Great Britain

Contents

Acknowledgements

There are so many people we wish to thank for their help in compiling this book and we have been overwhelmed by the enthusiasm that they all showed when relating their stories. Our very grateful thanks go to:

Ada Beckett, Angela and Dennis Eggleton, Ann and Dave Allworth, Barbara and John Williams, Barbara Richer, Barbara Wharton, Betty and Dave Pinfold, Brian Way, Eunice Clifford, Freda Ackroyd, Gillian Wootton, Gordon Todd, Harold Mitchell, Janet Preston, Jean Stevens, Joan and Nigel Fountain, Joyce King, Julie Beckingham, Marion and Colyn Makepeace, Maureen and Jim Cairney, Pete Boland, Roland Attridge, Shelagh Baker, Sue Attridge and Sylvia and Ron Wynands.

And thanks also to the many other people who have chipped in with bits of information and detail.

We would also like to convey our sincere thanks to all those Princes Risborough folk sadly no longer with us, who contributed so much to the town, and without whom much of this book would not have been possible.

And finally, if you have been inspired by this book to record your memories and anecdotes, then we would like to continue collecting material for the Risborough Heritage Society Archives. We would like to hear from you and you can contact the authors for further details by email at: mpayne233@btopenworld.com.

Picture Credits

Many of the pictures in this book are taken from the private collections of the people of Princes Risborough. We have taken every care to verify the copyright of each photograph, but if any copyright permission has been inadvertently overlooked then we apologise and ask forgiveness. The following have kindly allowed their own photographs to be used and we sincerely thank them:

Nigel Fountain, Ada Beckett, John Williams, Barbara Richer, Ron and Sylvia Wynands, Freda Ackroyd, Maureen Cairney, The Bucks Free Press, The Payne family, Pete Boland, Colyn and Marion Makepeace, Tom Gilmour, The Attridge Family, Dennis Eggleton, Barbara Wharton, Eunice Clifford, Dave Pinfold, Harold Mitchell, Gordon Todd and Jean Stevens.

We would also like to thank Graham Payne for his help in preparing the photos for publication.

Introduction

In October 2008, we were to reach our Ruby wedding anniversary and by way of celebration, one of the things we wanted to do was to record some of the memories of our lives together, living in Princes Risborough. We were married in St Mary's Church in 1968, and all our married life we have lived and worked in the town.

When we sat down to start to record our thoughts, we decided to enlist some help from our friends and acquaintances, and they were all only too pleased to relate their own stories. We have had many pleasant evenings reminiscing about the life and times of Princes Risborough with them and so many previously unpublished stories and anecdotes have been uncovered.

We made a decision to have a cut-off point, and the story really begins at the outbreak of the Second World War. It is probably fair to say that Risborough has changed more in the period since 1939 than at any other time in its long history as a settlement. We also decided to concentrate on people's memories rather than the architecture or the layout of the town, although this has been touched upon many times in the conversations. We wanted to record the quirky episodes from people's lives, the fun and laughter that has always been predominant here, the serious and sad times, and the stories that our children, and our children's children, will be able to recount about this famous Chilterns town for many years to come. We were concerned that one day these stories would be lost forever, so we were determined to record them for future generations.

Angela has lived here for virtually all of her life and Michael has now been here for three-quarters of his, but it has been an amazing experience to find out just how much we didn't know about Princes Risborough and its people.

We hope that you will join us in this journey down memory lane and find it as fascinating as we did.

Michael and Angela Payne
October 2009

Chapter One

Developing from Village to Town

Over the years, thanks to sterling work from local historians like Chris Kingham and Sandy McFarlane, Princes Risborough's history has been well documented, especially in pictorial form. But for this book we wanted to talk to the people who actually lived and worked in the town throughout the last sixty to seventy years. We have spoken to lots of people who have lived in and around Risborough for most of their lives and in these pages we want to recount their memories and to give you a feel of how different life was for the population of one of Buckinghamshire's busiest small towns. I think you will find, as you read on, a treasure trove of memories has been unearthed which will give a real insight into how the town has evolved during that time.

As we all know life was so different for everyone back in the 1930s, '40s and '50s. Growing up was so much slower and children had the time to be children for much longer than they seem to nowadays. It is fair to say that just after the war, Princes Risborough was more of a large village rather than a town and a much different place to live in than it is today. But it also had a great deal to offer, both for shopping and also for social events. More importantly, it had the potential to develop.

After the Second World War ended, the town grew to a much larger size and new estates began to appear in what were previously open fields and marshlands.

John Williams and his wife Barbara, and Barbara's sister Maureen and her husband, Jim Cairney, have lived in and around the town for all of their lives. Although to be precise, it was Monks Risborough and Longwick during their childhood years. John and Barbara still live in the same cottage on the Aylesbury Road, Monks Risborough, which John grew up in. John recalls, 'My Mum was born in the cottage next door and she also eventually died there as well, and my grandfather used to have a blacksmith shop next door to that, a building that is still there today. We never went far in those days.' Betty Pinfold, who was also born in Monks Risborough, has many memories of her childhood and of the blacksmiths, 'I remember going to school with John Williams and when it was conker time we used to go round to John's and he would fetch some big horse nails from the blacksmiths to pierce our conkers ready for the string to be threaded through.'

Horse and cart in Kingsmead.

As sisters, Maureen and Barbara lived in Kingsmead, and Maureen remembers that half the road was built before the war and the other half was built after the war, 'We were not far from Risborough, but a lot of people in the town didn't even know Kingsmead existed! But we were a really close-knit community there and everyone helped each other.' In those days the Westmead and Place Farm estates of today were just fields, and the girls remember how they used to tramp across those fields to go to town, 'It was just fields and watercress beds with streams running across the land, you nearly always needed your wellies!' John remembers how it began to change, 'My house backed on to Burton Lane but beyond that there was nothing but fields and streams. Wellington Avenue was the first road built on that land, in the late 1950s I think, and the estate sort of grew from that.'

It was the same story on the other side of town as the Berryfield Road estate gradually grew and grew. John continues, 'It was the early 1950s when the Woodfield, Southfield and Eastfield roads were built and the Ash Road estate also sprang up. They were all originally council properties so it meant a large influx of people either came into the town or moved from other rented properties in the county. It certainly changed the town forever.'

There was also a new private housing estate built, again on land that was formally fields and wasteland, and this was called Stratton Road. Again, lots of new people came to the town, which meant the amenities had to grow with the population. More of that later...

One of the biggest developments came with the arrival from Deptford, London, of the Molins Tobacco Machinery Company based on a purpose-built site at Saunderton, just four miles from the town. It was to be a major employer of Risborough people for the next fifty years and also would have a profound effect on the housing in the town. Fairway, off Station Road, was built by Molins to help house the workers who moved with the company from Deptford in London. Molins also bought many more properties in and around Risborough, so much so that at one point the company actually employed a housing manager to oversee all the buildings they owned. It was only later that the occupants of those houses were given the chance to buy them from the company. Many people took advantage of what proved to be some very good deals.

Working at Molins was pretty good for thousands of people as our co-author Mike Payne reveals:

> In the old days Molins were one of the best companies in the country to work for. Desmond Molins was first and foremost an engineer and the products he helped develop were way ahead of their time. The expertise and precision was second to none and many young Risborough lads did their apprenticeship at Molins and then went on to become highly skilled engineers. And the fun that we had there was also unforgettable, with so many stories to be told about the amazing characters that worked at the site. Until recent years the management at Molins were all steeped in Molins history and prided themselves on the high levels of precision and skill that the company demanded. When I started in 1973, there were 1,500 people on that site. We had subsidised travel from Risborough with a fleet of coaches bringing the workforce in from all around the area. We had a subsidised canteen, a nurse on site, a terrific sports and social club in Monks Risborough, and plenty of job opportunities within the company. It is one of the saddest things that has ever happened to the town of Princes Risborough, seeing that fine company dwindle away to almost nothing. Desmond would be turning in his grave.

In the early 1950s there was a lot of good employment in and around the town. Cheverton and Laidler's had been established since the 1920s: Risborough Furniture, Enfield

Berryfield Road before the estate was built.

Buckinghamshire Education Committee
Wycombe Divisional Executive

OFFICIAL OPENING

OF THE

Princes Risborough
County Secondary School

Friday, 6th December, 1957
at 7.0 p.m.

By
J. W. MOSS, ESQ.

CHAIRMAN :
THE REV. E. ELLIS ROBERTS, M.C., M.A.
Chairman of the School Governors

The opening of the Top School.

Bell Street School.

New Road Hill.

Upholstery, Austin Hoy, Ortho's, the Forest Laboratory and lots of smaller shops and businesses. They were all very good companies and it was not unusual for people to work for over twenty, thirty and sometimes over forty years at the same place. There was also a busy railway station, a Police Station, a Fire Brigade, a doctor's and several schools, so finding work was not such a problem for the many new people arriving in the town after the war.

In the late 1950s the Secondary Modern School, affectionately known as 'the Top School', was built at the end of Clifford Road and Merton Road. Pupils had earlier completed their secondary education at the Bell Street School, but now the new generation of children had a modern complex that was to revolutionise Princes Risborough schooling. An annexe was also opened in Berryfield Road and there the pupils would learn about domestic science and rural science. That part of the school later became Berryfield School for younger children. There was also Berndene on Wellington Avenue and of course there were good schools at Monks Risborough and Longwick. These schools were all necessary for the growing town as from 1951 to 1971 the population of Princes Risborough more than doubled.

The other amenities available also changed with clubs and societies forming all over the town. We had a good library, plenty of sports clubs, Cubs, Scouts, Brownies and Guides, several excellent pubs and lovely natural facilities like the Whiteleaf Cross where walkers could enjoy the healthy air of the Chiltern Hills. We also had good travel links to High Wycombe, Aylesbury and, of course, London.

All in all Princes Risborough was becoming a good place to live.

Chapter Two

In Times of War

One of the most familiar faces in Princes Risborough over the past sixty or so years is Barbara Richer, but she wasn't born here. Instead, she arrived as a rather bemused ten-year-old little girl in September 1940, sent here by her mother to escape the terrible bombing being inflicted on London at that time by the German Luftwaffe.

Barbara recalls:

> I was brought up living near Wimbledon Common and my school was on the common itself. After the Second World War started we felt the full brunt of the Blitz and my mother was very worried about keeping me at home. Lots of children were being evacuated to the country, but for a while I stayed in London. I remember one day a German aircraft swooped low over our home and machined gunned the street below. Five children were killed that awful day. The event prompted the authorities to dig a long trench across the Common from the school and away from the area. They hoped that, if it happened again, then at least people would be able to dive in the trench for cover. As it turned out though the school was closed shortly afterwards and all my friends and I became street urchins. We would often spend whole nights in our Anderson shelter in the garden and then, the next day, we would sift through all the destruction to see who could find the biggest piece of shrapnel.

In the end the danger became too great in London and Barbara's mother had a friend who knew a family who lived in the country. The family that took the Londoner under their wing turned out to be the Watermans, who lived in a house in Wycombe Road, Princes Risborough. Mr and Mrs Waterman had one daughter, Joan, and she was to become a lifelong friend to the young Barbara. In June 1941 Joan married Ernie Morris, a butcher from the town, and that marriage would change Barbara's life forever.

It did however take a while for Barbara to settle into country life, especially as she had had to leave her mother in war-ravaged London. But gradually she adapted to life in her new surroundings, so much so that she eventually stayed in the town for good!

A young Barbara Richer.

To be honest, I think I was a country girl at heart, and I really fell in love with Risborough from the beginning. Mr and Mrs Waterman were very kind to me, I called them 'Pop' and 'Nan'. My own Dad had died at just thirty-two years of age so I never really had time to get to know him. But 'Pop' Waterman made me feel so welcome, he even gave me a corner of his garden to plant up. I was so excited to see the plants grow. We never had much by way of entertainment in those days, although we did make our own. In the winter though you never went out much, we would stay in the warm and read or sometimes listen to the wireless. One of the best attractions at the time, although I wasn't allowed to go, was Saturday nights at the Walsingham Hall. Apparently it was quite a dive with dances and allsorts. There was a games room at the back, for table tennis and card games, etc. And of course the other big thing in the town was the Carlton Cinema! That was very popular and they used to change the film twice a week.

Life in wartime Risborough was much like it was in the rest of the country, with food scarce, people frightened and everyone on alert. But the community was so close-knit. Everyone knew everyone else and if anyone had problems they knew they could rely on their neighbours to help. Barbara recalls:

We all made the best of things. To give you an example, Pop used to work at the Forest Products Laboratory and occasionally they would have students and experts come over to study all the latest wood techniques, preservation, etc., etc. One girl, who stayed with us, came

The Walsingham Hall.

over for about three months from her home in South Africa. When she went home she sent me some wool, something you couldn't buy here at the time. You can imagine how thrilled I was. It was two-ply wool and I carefully knitted it into a nice garment. I was so proud of it, but two years later I then carefully unpicked the whole thing before knitting another garment to wear!

Barbara also remembers a Mr Angood who ran what can only be described as an emporium, a shop where the Chinese takeaway is now at Wycombe Road:

Mr Angood sold everything in that shop and he would come round to the house taking orders from the back of his van. Nan would ask him if he had anything 'special' this week? By that she meant anything that wasn't rationed! Mr Angood would say, 'Well, yes, I can let you have a penny packet of custard powder this week, or two boxes of matches, or a little packet of starch perhaps.' It was wonderful if he had some biscuits!

There was a Home Guard unit in the town and Barbara remembers:

The blackout rules were very strictly enforced. We would sometimes see the odd rogue German aircraft fly over, probably on its way home from a raid on one of the big cities. I distinctly remember an unexploded bomb being found at the bottom of Clifford Road. The Home Guard manned lookouts at a pillar-box at the top of what is now Culverton Hill. It was in a perfect position to see across the valley, towards the station, and then beyond towards Chinnor. The remains of that pillar-box can still be seen today. They also had a lookout station at the top of the Whiteleaf Cross, for obvious reasons. Occasionally, other strange things also happened in Risborough during the war. One day some men arrived in a lorry at the Post Office. Guards were mounted as a large number of gold bars were unloaded and stored in an upstairs room. That room was then sealed off for the duration of the war.

For a time Barbara moved in with Ernie and Joan Morris at their Saunderton home, and she actually finished her schooling at Bledlow Ridge School. When she left school as a fourteen-year-old she wanted to work in the butcher's shop but alas there was no vacancy at the time. But Barbara did manage to find a job working for the Norwich Union. The huge insurance company had also come out of London at the height of the Blitz, moving their offices from Piccadilly, Fleet Street and St James's out to the country, away from the bombing. Where did they set their business up? At Horsenden Manor no less, now home to Risborough's most famous resident, Jay Kay! The Norwich Union used the stables, with the downstairs being the telephone exchange and the upstairs used as the stationary stores.

Barbara worked for the Norwich Union for about a year:

I remember that me and the other girls from the town who worked there formed a kind of Girl's Brigade. We would dress up in our uniform of blue skirts, white blouses and forage caps and then march up and down Back Lane. We had no arms or armour so I don't know what the hell we thought we were doing! We would probably have run a mile if anything had happened! Still, I suppose we thought we were doing our bit for the war effort.

Ernie and Joan Morris's wedding day at St Mary's Church.

At the end of the war, the Norwich Union moved back to their London base and Barbara was out of a job. Luckily, there was now a vacancy at the butchers as Barbara Wharton had left to join another butcher in the town, although she would later train as a nurse, a role she was to make her own in the Cross Keys surgery for many years after. The other Barbara, meanwhile, was to start her new career:

> Although the people of Princes Risborough primarily remember me from serving in the shop kiosk, that came much later. When I first started in the shop I was so shy that if a man came in I wouldn't serve him! But Ernie Morris was to teach me all the butchery skills and I spent most of my time carving up the carcasses that arrived from the farm. It was an excellent skill for me to learn and even today I'm pretty sure I could cut some perfect joints from the beef, pork or lamb. I sometimes look at today's supermarket cuts and raise my eyes to the heavens in disgust!

Petrol was very scarce during the war years, and only a few selected people were given a special licence allocating them a small supply for their work. Doctors for instance, and also certain businessmen, were granted a licence. Barbara's guardian, Mr Waterman, had his allowance for fuel because of his role as Fire Officer at the Forest Products Laboratory in Summerleys Road, where he worked. And Ernie Morris was also given a supply for his two butchery vans. Those vans became an essential sight for many people in the town and in the outlying villages such as Saunderton, Loosley Row, Lacey Green, Longwick, and so on. Ernie ran his butchers with his brothers, Dick and Ralph. Ernie ran the shop, Dick was the buyer of the various animals for the farm and Ralph ran the farm, supplying the

The Forest Laboratory's Fire Brigade.

Ernie Morris (right) on a rabbit shoot.

shop with the meat. They ran the butchers under their father's name, Walter James Morris, hence the sign above the shop that remained for many years, 'W.J. Morris & Sons'.

Barbara recalls:

We really provided an essential service for the community. Ernie's vans would deliver vital food to those people who could not get into the shop. Few people had cars in those days, and those that did had no petrol for weeks on end. And the families would all be glad of anything that Ernie could deliver. Even bags of bones or a little bit of fat would be warmly welcomed as they could make a tasty stew or something like that. We were lucky too that Ernie was allowed to shoot the rabbits on his farmland and then bring them to the shop. Blimey! Once news went around the town that Ernie had some rabbits in the shop, the Risborough folk went mad for them. Rabbits were a really good meal for many people during the war, but they were scarce, so a sight for sore eyes when they were available. Mind you, it was the same in Gillingwater's fruit shop further down the High Street. When they occasionally managed to receive a shipment of bananas and the town found out, the people descended on the shop in their droves!

When Barbara first worked at the butchers, the shop was on the corner of the High Street and Horns Lane. Next door was a large house, once a hotel, and then next to that was another large house. One familiar sight for Barbara and the people of Risborough in those wartime days was to see farmer Stan Woods herd his dairy cows from his farmyard off the Market Square, up through the High Street and on to his fields off to the left of New Road. She remembers it well:

Stan used to set his cows off up the street after milking, but used to stay with one particular cow that had deformed hooves. Stan would slowly walk with his bicycle alongside her, whilst the rest of the herd would go on ahead. When the herd reached the top of the High Street they would automatically turn left, and then right, into New Road. Bearing in mind that there was no Berryfield, Woodfield, Southfield or Eastfield Road housing estate in those days,

Stan Woods's cattle herd in the Market Square.

in fact it was just fields. Stan had two fields, an upper field and a lower field. Amazingly, it was the cows themselves that chose the field that they would go into, mainly because Stan was still escorting 'old dodgy feet' up the High Street! The farmer would arrive later and shut the gate to whichever field the cows had chosen.

Another story about that herd of cows still makes Barbara chuckle to this day:

We used to have a cheeky chap who worked with us in the butchers, Bert Tapping his name was. Bert used to prop open the shop door on hot days and as he did so on this very hot day, he saw Stan's herd coming up the High Street. As they drew level with the shop he whacked his axe down sideways on to the meat-cutting block. The loud bang startled the cows and they stampeded in all directions! After about an hour the cows were eventually all rounded up. Stan was not amused! He always spoke with a slight stammer and he came into the butchers, glared at us and said, 'I s-s-s-suppose you think that was b-b-b-bloody f-f-funny!' Poor old Stan!

During the war Pettigrove's Fair was based in the field, which is now the Horns Lane car park. One day the fair lost one of its most famous characters. When old Granny Pettigrove died, they certainly gave her a special send off. Barbara recalls:

I shall never forget the day of her funeral as even allowing for the austerity of the time, the wreaths were incredible. They stretched from St Mary's Church through the Market Square and right up the whole of the High Street. There were no florists then, but the display of flowers was unbelievably spectacular. Because Granny Pettigrove was a member of the Showman's Guild, that whole community did her proud with an amazing send off.

There was another wartime story about that field, which is now the site of the Marks & Spencer store, and it came near to where the newspaper shop door is today. Barbara remembers:

Just inside a large gate, where the newspaper shop is now, there used to be an old shed stored with oil and petrol. One day, an old Irishman, I never really knew who he was, or where he came from, staggered up to this shed in a rather drunken state. He was looking for somewhere to sleep for the night. He thought the shed would be an ideal place, and it would have been had he not lit a cigarette! The whole lot blew up. A few of us managed to pull the old man out and we eventually laid him out on to Ernie and Joan Morris's kitchen table. The doctor was called and he came quickly, but sadly there was nothing he could do, as the old man's burns were too severe. He died a few hours later.

Barbara eventually worked in the butchers for fifty years and she was to see many changes in that time, not only in the butchers but also in Princes Risborough as well. Mind you, she almost never made it through those fifty years, as this next story will tell you:

After the war was over Ernie's business grew and grew. In fact it outgrew the premises we were in so he decided to do something about it. Eventually he was able to buy the whole building and then he had it all knocked down and the present Morris House on the corner was built. That was in 1955 and it certainly caused a storm in the town, that's for sure, as many people objected to the proposal. But Ernie was a determined character and he finally won them round. He also had a wicked sense of humour too! When the rebuilding work was going on we carried on trading with a tarpaulin over us. How we got away with it I don't know, what with all the meat and foodstuffs around. You certainly wouldn't be allowed to do that today that's for sure! Anyway, one day we had this terrific rainstorm and flash floods. Ernie asked me to go into the big cold room we had at the time to fetch a pig's heart. So I came out with it and was a bit puzzled as to why he hadn't picked it up earlier. He then told me that when he tried to pick it up he received an electric shock and was surprised I didn't receive one! Charming, and normally such a nice man too! The rain continued to lash down and by now it was seeping down the sides of the tarpaulin. We carried on with our regular Saturday afternoon job of washing down all the chopping blocks and work surfaces. As we were working my leg brushed up against a galvanised bucket and I, too, received a shock. With that we sent over to the electricians, which was later Teleline, and asked Les Simmons the electrician to come and have a look. He put his meter on the shop window and found that even that was alive with electricity! The whole place was alive with it. Apparently all the rain water had seeped through a junction box and the place was a death trap!

Eventually the new building was completed as you see it today. On the corner the first tenant of the shop was a television firm called Wycombe Electrical, the butchers was in the middle and on the other end was the Chiltern Cleaners. There were also three lovely flats above the shops and for many years Barbara and husband Eric lived in one of them. They had married in 1959.

Later Barbara was to become a prominent member of the Town Council. In fact it was Ernie Morris who persuaded her to stand for election. She stood as an independent candidate and was one of the first people to be voted on to the Council as opposed to being co-opted onto it. Altogether she spent thirteen years on the committee. She also became a leading member of the Princes Risborough Women's Institute and has now been involved in that for around forty years.

Barbara was very close to the Morris family, and still is, and she thought the world of her former boss, describing him as the best boss anyone could have. He was a perfect gentleman, had a wonderful sense of humour, loved joking with his staff and customers and yet never once raised his voice in anger. Mind you, he did make a point when he sharpened his knives on his blade. Barbara recalls:

> You could always guess when you had to stop mucking about and get on with your work, just by his look and the way he sharpened those knives! But he was a wonderful man who cared very much about the people of the community.

When we asked Barbara what she missed most about those early days in Princes Risborough she said:

> People had time for one another and family life prevailed. We knew all the children of each family and if they were ill we would worry about them. We all knew and cared about each other and there was a super community spirit. Sadly, much of that has now gone.

Chapter Three

The Shops of Princes Risborough – 'The Golden Years'

Everyone we have spoken to remember the shops of Princes Risborough in the late 1950s and early 1960s with a mixture of warm fondness and a touch of sadness at the passing of some rare establishments. We wanted to highlight the variety and the individuality of the shops Risborough had back in those days, so we thought we would start on the left at the bottom of Duke Street and work our way up to the top of Bell Street and back down the other side of the road. With the help of our many interviewees, and especially John Williams, we have tried to piece together a picture of the shops and shopkeepers who have graced the town, concentrating on the period between 1950 and the mid-1960s. Apologies in advance for any mistakes or omissions, but just see how many of these shops you can remember.

The first shop was Turners, a leather and sports shop, then came Bloss's haberdashery and old Mrs Lacey's builders merchants. John Williams remembers:

> Mrs Lacey was about 100 years old when I was a kid, or at least she seemed that old, and her shop was an emporium of screws and nails and bits and pieces, it was always fascinating to go in there. Eventually it was taken over by Mr Kibble and was the forerunner of Kibble's hardware shop. There was a chap who worked in there, called Reg Crew, who was a Risborough fireman, but also made the coffins for Mr Kibble's undertaker business.

In the early 1960s there was a music shop called Purcells in this end of Duke Street. At the time, pop music was seeing the birth of The Beatles and many more groups from that extraordinary period. Many of the young teenagers who lived in Risborough then would have almost certainly bought their first records in Purcells. Co-author Mike Payne recalls:

> There was so much going on in the music world when we were growing up and Purcells was my first stop each week after I was paid. I was a big Roy Orbison fan [I still am!] and as I searched through the singles in Purcells, I was delighted if I found a new record Roy had released. But The Beatles were also just taking the world by storm and the shop could never

DUKE STREET, PRINCES RISBOROUGH.

The Shop for value for Money.

Ꮓ Bloss & Sons

DRAPERS, CLOTHIERS, & BOOT FACTORS,

A large and well assorted Stock
of Reliable Goods in all Departments.

Bucks Lace. — A choice assortment of Pillow Lace
Handkerchief Borders, Lace Collars etc.
Made in the surrounding villages.

Tailoring Dept. — A Large selection of the newest
patterns in Suitings, Trouserings & Overcoatings.

A Speciality — Our 30/- Suit to measure.
Style, Fit, and Workmanship Guaranteed.

Local Depot for **Achille Serre, Ltd.**

HIGH CLASS CLEANERS & DYERS.
Goods despatched Daily

Bloss's advert.

get enough of their new singles! And then there was The Rolling Stones, Elvis, The Hollies, The Animals and countless other top bands. My wife Angela also bought her first record in Purcells, 'Bits and Pieces' by the Dave Clark Five! An amazing music time.

Next along Duke Street was Jeffries the butchers, which stayed a butchers shop for many years, although with different owners. Then came the shop that everyone remembers with great affection, Adcock & Percival's. The shop was divided into toys and newspapers on one side, and groceries on the other. Upstairs Mr Adcock sold prams and also had a large Hornby model train layout. Maureen Cairney remembers:

We all bought our first prams there! The smell of coffee beans in the grocery part was another vivid memory and the wooden floorboards throughout the shop creaked as you walked on them. As kids we would take our birthday money into Adcocks and find a toy or game to buy.

John remembered how he did a paper round for Mr Adcock:

I used to get 9s per week, with an extra shilling for using my own bike! I started my round at the bottom of Risborough Hill, at the doctor's [now Wellington House] and I would have to do all along the Aylesbury Road, including Queen's Road, and do about ninety houses! Nowadays the kids get about £30 to do about ten houses! We used to have these big old leather bags that weighed a ton, even heavier when it rained.

Mr Copcutt's kiosk on the railway station.

Maureen added that when she did a paper round at Adcocks she used the shop bike, a big heavy contraption with a metal basket on the front.

Our co-author Angela Payne recalls:

A memory of Adcocks that I have came when our Mum used to take my sisters and me to the shop near Christmas and ask us to choose a present we would like. Mum wouldn't buy them then but would go back later on her own to buy the things we wanted, as long as they weren't too dear, and then take them home and hide them in her wardrobe. We were naughty because when Mum went out we would dash upstairs and search the wardrobe to see if she had bought the present we wanted. It ruined the surprise at Christmas, but it was very exciting.

Jim Cairney weighed in with his paper round story at this point, although his was a slightly different one as it wasn't with Adcocks:

I lived at Longwick at the time and used to cycle from home to the railway station and pick up the papers from Copcutts, a little kiosk on the station. I would then have to go back to Longwick and deliver the papers along the whole length of the village!

The shop next to Adcocks was a grocers, called Walker's Stores. This would serve the Brooke Road, Cannon Place and Wellington Avenue end of Risborough before the big Tesco store came to town. Walker's Stores eventually moved to where the larger Lloyds the chemist is now and later became Key Markets. There was a gap after Walker's Stores where

The Market Square, 1947.

The Copper Urn.

the old Risborough Brewery used to be and then came a ladies hairdressers called Ruby Hurren. Ruby and her team created many a posh hairdo, and later she opened another hairdressers above the Corner Shop in the Market Square, this time calling it Rosemary's.

If sewing or knitting was your pastime, then the Silver Wool Shop would cater for most of your needs. Barclay's Bank then came next, with a dentist in between the bank and the George & Dragon pub. The former coaching stop-off from days gone by has been on the same site for several hundred years now and is still one of the most familiar buildings in the town.

John and Barbara Williams both recall a small café called the Copper Urn. Barbara says:

> It was a good meeting place for the teenagers of the day, and many a romance began there.
> It was also a meeting place for the Teddy Boys and some of the lads had all the gear, the
> drainpipe trousers, big pumps, large jackets and of course the haircuts!

The doctor's surgery, the Cross Keys, was still where it is today but was very different in those days. We had Dr Edwards, Dr Cooper, Dr Gould and Dr Fordham as the practitioners, and everyone knew who their doctor was. Dr Edwards and Dr Cooper were founder members of the practice and their influence was to be the blueprint for many years to come. John recalls, 'There was also a doctor's practice in Duke Street, in the cottage next to where the cycle shop is today, that was run by a Dr Leviticus and a Dr Reidy. Later they were to bring in Dr Sandy McFarlane, and the Wellington House Surgery was eventually set up.'

Moving on up the High Street, next to the Cross Keys Surgery, you had Wainwright's shoe shop. Mr Wainwright and his ancestors have been on this site since the nineteenth

Padley's, Wainwright's and the Cross Keys.

century. At one time there was a small delicatessen between the surgery and the shoe shop, but that eventually closed and it became part of Wainwright's. Padley & Binns the chemist came next and the shop is still a chemist to this day (Lloyds). Most people of a certain age still refer to it as 'Padley's' though, and it was certainly handy for the surgery.

Padley's was the first of a trio of shops that stayed the same for many years. Next door was a greengrocers called Gillingwater's and then came a bakery, called Steel's. Those three busy shops served the community for many years together and not only did they provide a terrific service, they also became the source of employment for many people of the town. The three shops stretch back to the war years and although new owners came in, those shops traded continuously until recent years when we sadly lost the greengrocers and bakers.

George Ellis was a familiar name for many years in Princes Risborough. He had a furniture and carpet store where the charity shop is now. Barbara remembers her Mum buying some furniture from Mr Ellis and co-author Angela Payne remembers buying the first fitted carpet she ever had from Mr Ellis. 'We bought it on HP and we went in every week religiously to make our payment. Mr Ellis would mark our HP card and it was always a great thrill when we finished our payments. Mind you, at a few shillings a week it seemed to take forever!'

The next shop was another café, this time called Granny's Pantry. Originally the tearooms were in the corner of the Market Square, but moved up to the High Street in the mid-1960s. The shop was one of the most popular in the town. Affectionately known as 'Granny's', it was run by a lady called Miss Coughlin, who later became Mrs Morris, and was along the lines of the old-fashioned Lyons Corner Houses of the war years. Lovely homemade cakes and light snacks and lunches kept the place very busy. Some of the staff were also stalwart Risborough folk, characters in their own right, such as Peggy Orchard, Ivy Mitchell, Joan Mathieson, Joan Payne and Wendy Lewis. It was a good place to work and is one of the most missed shops from the era.

Next to Granny's was a pet shop and a small ladies clothes shop called E & H's. 'We used to buy all our stockings at E & H's,' recalls Angela, 'and I distinctly remember everything in the shop was in a drawer.' Next to those two shops there was a solicitor's office called Lightfoot & Lownes and then for a long time there was a large house. John remembers, 'Eventually that house was demolished and they built a Co-op supermarket. The Co-op was actually split into three shops, the supermarket, an electrical store and then a Co-op chemist. Upstairs there were several nice flats, mainly occupied by staff.'

Again the Co-op proved an excellent employer for the town. Managed by Ted Janes or Ron Hoyle, the staff became a who's who of familiar Risborough faces. Amongst others there were Sheila Small, Linda Madgwick, Marge Moseley, Hazel Rogers and Gladys Johnson, and later came Shelagh Attridge, Dawn Robinson, Mary Jones and a host of others. They were all real characters and there were many laughs had by all. Co-author Mike Payne began as a trainee manager there in 1966:

I worked for the Co-op for over five years, not always in Risborough, but that is where I started. I remember we used to have to put people's orders together, box them up, and deliver them around the town. One day Hazel Rogers came with me in the old Bedford van to deliver some groceries to a house in Meadle. When we arrived I fetched the big box from

Gillingwater's.

Joan Payne and Joan Mathieson
at Granny's Pantry.

The staff at Granny's, Joan Payne, Miss Coughlan, Joan Mathieson, Peggy Orchard, Ivy Mitchell and Pam Goodchild.

The Co-op.

the back of the van and walked down this path to the house. I was then confronted by two of the biggest and fiercest dogs you have ever seen, barking and growling their heads off! Hazel, meanwhile, had stayed in the van. She slammed her door shut and sat laughing like a drain at my predicament. To say I was terrified would be an understatement and I really thought my last sight on this earth was to see Hazel laughing! The lady from the house came out and said those immortal words that do no good at all to a person who hates dogs, 'They won't hurt you!' She took the box from my shaking hands and I backed off gingerly towards the safety of the van and a guffawing Hazel. It took me years to get over that and yet Hazel is still laughing about it to this day!

Many years ago the next building in the High Street was a hotel, but that was demolished in 1955 and Morris House was built. The Chiltern Cleaners took the first shop in the block, Morris's the butchers took the middle one and the first tenant of the end shop was Wycombe Electrical, a television and electrical goods supplier. Again, above those shops were three excellent flats. The co-author again recalls:

When I first came to Princes Risborough, I lived in the end flat, over Wycombe Electrical, where my Dad, Dan, had found a job. We loved that flat as it had the perfect view as to all that went on in the town. I remember we had a great view on the night of the fire when the old Carlton Cinema went up, and I recall watching all the people running along the street in their pyjamas to see what was going on! But my vivid memory of living at Morris House is of the shop below. I am a big football fan and at the time *Match of the Day* was starting up on BBC TV. Unfortunately, the programme was first broadcast on BBC Two and we didn't have the new station on our telly. So my brother Graham and I arranged with Tom Lunnon, then manager of Wycombe Electrical, to set his time switches to make sure the televisions in the shop came on for the start of *Match of the Day*. Graham and I would then go downstairs and stand on the pavement outside and watch the football! It was snowing one night whilst we were stood there, so we took a flask of hot tea! The only sad thing was we couldn't hear Kenneth Wolstenholme's commentary.

Joyce (Attridge) King has a memory of the same shop after it became Lloyd's Electrical:

I remember working there for a while, next to Morris's the butchers. Barry Clark and the boys in there were always winding me up and playing tricks on me. I remember once, the phone rang and the voice said, 'It's the GPO here. We have reason to believe that there is a danger your phone is about to catch fire, can you put the receiver into a bucket of water please?' Of course, me being me, like an idiot, I did exactly what they told me to do. I could have throttled Barry when I realised it was him mucking about again!

Around the corner from Morris House was Jack Newitt's sand and ballast yard. Jack's lorries trundled around the town for many years driven by people like Sam Tucker, Tom Warner, John Williams and Les Payne. They would ferry backwards and forwards to the quarries over at Leighton Buzzard and then deliver all around the area. It was a hive of activity for many years and again, Jack was another solid employer for the Risborough

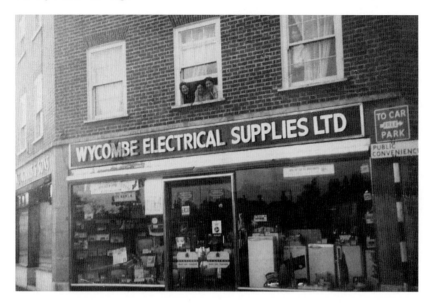

Wycombe
Electrical
Ltd.

workforce. At that time of course the route through Risborough went straight down the High Street and not along Horns Lane as it does now.

Opposite Jack Newitt's yard was once just fields, but then a car park was put in to serve the town. There were no shops where Marks & Spencer is now and the first building in Bell Street was then the White Lion pub. Maureen Cairney remembers how foul the toilets in that car park used to be, 'They stunk to high heaven and they were filthy!' She also remembers that, years before, the local scouts used to camp on the wasteland there and also that Pettigroves fair would use the site for their quarters. 'It was not unusual to see a goat and a donkey tethered on that piece of land either.'

So, moving along Bell Street, you then had Luxton's fruit and vegetable shop and George Nicholls's gentlemans hairdressers. Next door to that was a grocers called Dorset's. That grocery store later changed to become Anthony Jackson's and then a Victor Value shop, before later becoming the first Tesco in Risborough. After the entrance to the Baptist Chapel there was a shop called Lydia Carter, a ladies beauty and make-up shop. Maureen and Barbara both remember having their ears pierced at Lydia Carter's.

The cottages after Lydia Carter were mainly residential for many years, although another gent's hairdressers was opened in 1964 by Wally Burton, in the shop that was Eggleton's the bakers and is now a florist. Wally, a Lancastrian who married a Risborough girl, was one of the most likeable men to ever live in the town. Many of today's adults had their first haircuts at Wally Burton's shop. Always friendly, always a gentleman and always smiling, Wally had time to listen to all of your trials and tribulations, just like a good barber should! And his work was never finished after the shop shut at the end of the day. Wally would visit countless customers who were unable to make it into the shop, and cut their hair in their own homes. It was often very late when he finally got home. When the shop next door became available in 1965, Wally opened a toyshop, and it was run by his eldest daughter, and named 'Angela's' after her. The co-author of this book remembers it well, although sadly it was not to operate for very long:

Wally Burton, gentleman hairdresser.

Dad and I had problems getting permission to sell certain toys as there were rules in those days about competing with other shops that also sold those same toys. As we had Adcocks in the town it restricted our stock range and in the end we closed. The irony for me though was that it was my first proper job after leaving school, and my last job ended some forty-two years later, when I retired as manager of Treats 2 in Duke Street, which was of course a toyshop!

It is interesting to note that when the current owners of Wally's old shop, Fuller's Flowers, had the floor retiled, they found, under the old tiles, a well worn semi-circle around what had once been the base of Wally's customer chair. Obviously, for many years, as he cut people's hair, he was moving in the same spot, and it had worn the floor away! That worn patch is still there, now under the new tiles.

Moving on along Bell Street, the Jacobs Service Station and the Carlton Cinema came before the school. The cinema is fondly remembered in other parts of this book, but John Williams remembers going there regularly:

There was a Mrs Laverick who used to take our money at the ticket office. You could buy tickets for 1*s*, 1*s* 9*d*, 2*s* 3*d* and 3*s* 6*d* for the balcony! [For those of you under the age of thirty-seven reading this, those prices equate to 5p, 8½p, 11p and 17½p!] The shilling tickets were known as 'crawl-backs'. That was because when the lights went out you would sink down to the floor and crawl back under the seats back to the dearer rows! I also remember watching some great films when they first came out, like The Dambusters, Spartacus, and all the 'Doctor' comedy films. It was a sad day when the Carlton closed, and even sadder when it burnt down some years later.

Crossing the road from the cinema and Bell Street School you came to two shops, one of which, for several years, was Jason Abbott's Gun & Countryside shop. Next door to that

Bell Street shops.

The Carlton Cinema and the Bell Service Station.

A 1950s Princes Risborough fête, off Back Lane.

was a shop that holds many memories for nearly every schoolboy and schoolgirl that grew up in the 1950s and 1960s, Tiffany's sweet shop. This was the shop that many children over the years made a beeline for after school. It had a fine array of sweets and could satisfy the sweetest of teeth. You could get quite a lot for 'thruppence' then!

The British Legion club and the Post Office straddled Park Street. Back in the 1950s it was decided to build the British Legion Club. To help raise funds for the cost of this, the organisers held an annual fete in the field behind Back Lane, which is now the Retreat. Those fêtes were very popular and all the residents would turn out for them. They had some star attractions and even the Dagenham Girl Pipers appeared at one of the fêtes. When you see the photos of those fêtes it is good to see how everyone dressed smartly for them with all the young girls and boys in their Sunday best clothes.

Further along you came to one of the oldest pubs in the town, the Bell. Risborough has never been short of a pub or two! Between the pub and, what is now the library, has probably seen the most changes of all the shopping areas in the town during this period we are concentrating on. Just along from the Bell there was a long-serving grocer called Mr Redman who had a general grocery store. This was another shop with wooden flooring and distinctive smells from a large array of goods. There is something about the combination smells of firelighters and fresh bread, or soap powders and fresh vegetables, all in a relatively small area. Mr Redman knew where everything was though and he was the archetypal jolly grocer. There were other shops further along the road from Mr Redman, long since gone, but one was yet another gent's hairdressers, Gilbert Young.

John Williams remembers that hairdressers well:

It was there for years, and he even used to cut my Grandad's hair before the war! As young lads we always found it funny when Gilbert asked us if we wanted 'anything for the weekend?' It got to the point that everyone in the town referred to condoms as 'Gilbeys'!

The High Street, 1947.

Maureen Cairney also remembers the shop, and especially the fear of her brother, James, when she took him for a haircut. 'We got him in the chair and Gilbert put the smock around him. But when Gilbert turned round, James legged it, out the door, and down the High Street with me chasing him!'

Where the library is now used to be a builder's yard of some sort, but then back in the High Street there was another fine mixture of shops down this side too. For many years there was a big store called Barley's, which was a large chemist and drug store. Next door, Mr Boughton opened a unique service with his shop Teleline, a new idea in television with the channels being piped in through underground cables. He had an aerial station at the top of Kop Hill and although his cables could not reach every street, he certainly covered much of the town. It was an idea ahead of its time and kept Mr Boughton in business for many years.

One of the next shops along the street was one of the best and most charismatic of all the shops in the town, the ladies and gent's outfitters called Leslie Hermon. Advertising himself as 'The Shirt King', the shop was piled high with tops, shirts, underwear, trousers, socks, skirts, jeans, hats, ties and shoes. Somewhere hidden amongst the stock was Mrs Meredith, who always seemed to have her overcoat on when she served you! If you asked for a pair of pants she would fetch out box after box of them and pile them up on the counter until you found the pair you wanted. The trouble was that most of that stock on the counter would stay there and in the end, Mrs Meredith would be peering at you through this mountain of clothes! She knew where everything was though and could lay her hands on anything you wanted. Many a Mum kitted their children out from top to toe at Hermon's, and the shop is much missed.

Mr Kibble had his hardware shop next and again, that was a shop with a unique smell, with paraffin prevalent. Then came George Jacobs's High Street garage. There were petrol pumps in the street and a workshop and garage tucked away at the back. There was also a car showroom, and he sold bicycles as well. Co-author Angela recalls:

I bought a second-hand bike off Mr Jacobs before I left school. Dad gave me the deposit, but I had to pay back all the rest out of my pocket money, or from the money I earned from helping Dad in his shop [Wally Burton's]. I went down to Mr Jacobs every week without fail and paid him around 10s a week. I think the bike cost around £14 to start with. Anyway, I was so thrilled when I finally reached the last payment and bounded into Mr Jacobs's shop to give him the last 10s. Imagine my delight, then, when Mr Jacobs, who had been so impressed with how good I had been with the payments, told me that I could keep that last ten bob and that the bike was now mine! I loved that bike, it had a big basket on the front and I went everywhere on it, and I never ever forgot that touch of kindness from Mr Jacobs.

Moving along the High Street, the next shop was Dorothea's, a ladies fashion shop. Then came the Literary Institute, a building full of stories but a mystery to most of the people that lived in the town. At one time it was the local Magistrate's Court, but that had to be curtailed because of the instability of the floors. It was unable to sustain the weight of people wanting to be present at the trials. It later housed a snooker table for use by the members.

Next door was once another house, which was eventually converted into what was then the Westminster Bank, and then came Hestor's the jewellers. Lots of Risborough brides and grooms bought their wedding rings from Hestor's. Another ladies fashion shop called Anne's came next and there was, and is, an archway after that shop, which led to Mr Woods's farm at the back of the High Street. Appropriately, the next shop was the Askett Dairy, although later it was to become another greengrocers. Next door to that was a gent's outfitters called Frank Gray. This was a little more bespoke than Leslie Hermon's shop and you could buy a nice tailored suit from Mr Gray.

Another of the town's favourite shopkeepers was next along the street as Robin Ball's confectionery and tobacconist was a hive of activity amongst the locals. Robin had a cheery chat for everyone who climbed the couple of steps into his shop. He later sold a few toys and at one point he opened another similar shop in Bell Street called Judy's, which was indeed run by Judy, Robin's wife. They were a very popular couple in the town and Robin's recent death was a sad loss and the end of an era. But he did leave many memories for those that knew him.

Another ladies fashion shop came next called Pullens, although it also went under the name Vanity for a while. Risborough Dairy then had a shop and Gifford's the baker's was next door, before the estate agents, then called Gosling & Redway. Giffords did the best sausage rolls in the town, especially when they were hot, and when our co-author worked in the corner shop he and Robert Earle used to buy six nearly every day and eat three each!

The fish and chip shop has been there for many years and at one time, when run by the Montgomery family, they even had a small sit-down restaurant, which was very popular. The Whiteleaf pub was formerly Ferguson's wine shop and then the Victoria Wine shop before becoming the town's newest public house.

That was the last of the shops at that point but down into Church Square there was a yard that housed Annis's, a shop that was the forerunner for today's organic shops. They sold allsorts, from seed potatoes to bags of firewood. In the same yard there was Timothy

The Corner Shop and Mr Heath's.

East, the coal merchants, and at one point too, the Fire Station was based here. Opposite the entrance to St Mary's Church, Cheverton & Laidler had their main factory. But after they moved down to their Longwick Road site the factory in Church Square was taken over by Enfield Upholstery.

The Princes Risborough Library has occupied several sites over the years. At one time it was housed in the Market Square Tower, and then it moved into what is now a restaurant in Church Street. Of course it is now housed in the purpose-built building at the top of the High Street. Risborough has always provided a splendid library service and it is still one of the focal points of the town. But, back to the Market Square, and Mr Heath's hardware and DIY shop was yet another busy and popular premises. He sold everything you needed to decorate your home and one distinct memory was the wallpaper pattern books he had. They were huge and Mr Heath had trouble lifting them! Like many other shops mentioned in this chapter, Mr Heath's shop was another with a unique smell all of its own.

Next door to Mr Heath's was a newsagents and tobacconists. In the mid-1960s it was run by a Canadian, Martin Brunet, an unusual character who had many a tale to tell. In the shop he employed Mrs Bowler, a familiar Risborough face who knew most of what went on in the town, Robert Earle, son of Tom Earle of the Earle-Mitchell field fame, and our co-author Mike Payne. Mike recalls his old boss with affection:

Mr Brunet was a strange man, who looked a bit grumpy at times, but really he was a nice bloke who had a wicked sense of humour. He also had a number of surprising strings to his bow. I remember one night he asked if I would lock up for him as he had to leave early to attend to some business. Now bearing in mind that he had been in the shop since six o'clock that morning it came as some surprise to find out about the 'business' he was attending to. When he turned up for work the next morning he looked like death warmed up. I asked him if he was okay and he just said that he was a bit tired. I'm not surprised about that as it turned out that he had piloted a plane to Switzerland overnight to ferry a businessman there for a meeting! My other memory of Mr Brunet was of his wife, as she always came into the shop cuddling one of her Pekinese dogs!

We are nearly at the end of the shops now. As mentioned before, Granny's Pantry was once along the row behind the Market Tower, but that row has been either private residences or offices for many years now. Lloyds Bank has been on the corner at the top of Duke Street for many years too, although there are pictures of the building as a hotel in days gone by. Further down Duke Street the cottages have only been developed into shops over the past fifty years. John Sladen, another late, lamented stalwart Risborough shopkeeper, opened an unforgettable gift shop, called John's Ideas, where the toyshop was until recently. It was the sort of shop that suited the Risborough image and was in the Leslie Hermon mould. Every inch of floor space was crammed solidly with everything and anything suitable for a birthday present or wedding gift or the like. There was stock everywhere, but again, a real gem in Risborough's retail history.

Continuing down the last part of Duke Street, before Benyon's Garage, at one time there was another paper shop, Williams the butchers, Duval the greengrocer, Whitmee's fresh fish shop and A.J. Barrett's furniture store. Gill Wootton, née Attridge, had a great memory of Whitmee's fish shop:

That shop used to frighten me to death! It was always freezing cold and very dark when you went in there. Suddenly this lady would emerge from the back of the shop, stinking of fish and always wearing a long black overcoat. She had long, straggly hair and looked, well, to this youngster anyway, just like a witch! She was terrifying!

So there you are then, a period of time when the town was buzzing, the shops were busy and you were able to get everything you needed in Risborough's High Street. And there were also a few shops scattered around the town, which again did a brisk trade. In Poppy Road, for instance, there was the Parkfield Stores grocery shop and Woodfield Road also boasted a parade of shops. In Station Road you had Friday's the butchers and in Summerleys Road, there was another grocery store, Mr Adamson's chemist shop and next door to that there was Mr Adams's sweet shop, which he ran to supplement his insurance brokerage firm upstairs. There was also a garden tool shop in that row. When the Place Farm estate was built a parade of shops also served that estate, with a launderette doing particularly well.

In fact, there was something for everyone, in what can only be described as a golden age of shopping in Princes Risborough.

Chapter Four

Music, Music, Music

Pete Boland is another familiar character around Princes Risborough, and he has certainly played his part in shaping the local scene. Pete excelled in two fields, as a singer and as a football organiser. A strange combination, so let us explain.

The music scene in Princes Risborough has always had people willing to strut their stuff and from the war years onwards there has been some talented musicians living in and around the town. Around the mid-1950s a band founded by Jack Medway performed at local venues and very popular they were too. Pete Boland had moved down from his native Birmingham to live and work in High Wycombe at around that time and eventually joined Jack's band as the lead vocalist. Also in the band were Harold Henderson, Dave Purdom and Dave Farris, but after about four or five months Pete became a little disillusioned with the way the Jack Medway sound was going. Of course the late 1950s saw a huge change in musical tastes as rock and roll really started to shake the foundations of the music world. The advent of Elvis et al changed everything.

Pete recalls:

Jack's band was excellent and very popular, but I felt a little held back by the style. After the war the dance band was all the rage but gradually, as the 1950s progressed, people began to hear people like Elvis on the radio and the world went mad! I felt I wanted to do something just a little more exciting, so in the end I joined up with some other lads, Trevor Stott, Dickie French, Dave Simmons and another bloke from Bledlow, and we started another band. It was called The Wayfarers or something like that, but that band didn't last more than a few months and before long I was on the move again. When Harold Henderson, Dave Purdom and Dave Farris left the Jack Medway band they asked me if I would like to join them and so The Dave Peterson Four was born.

Now, whenever the name of the band came up it was fair to assume that Dave Peterson was one of the performers. Not so, in fact the name was derived from the band members, the two Daves (Purdom and Farris), Peter (Boland) and Son (from Harold Hender-son). 'We thought it was a clever idea at the time,' joked Pete.

Pete originally lived in High Wycombe and used to come over to Princes Risborough to meet up with his pals there. He was able to join the British Legion, thanks to his stint of National Service, and later he and his wife Jean had the chance to buy a bungalow on the brand new Westmead estate in Risborough. Pete says:

> In fact, we moved there in 1961 and it was the same week that the Carlton Cinema shut down. I remember that the original version of the film *Oceans 11* was on and it was free to go in during that last week. But we were so busy trying to sort out our new house that we never made it to the pictures.

It was in March 1962 that The Dave Peterson Four made their performing debut and Pete remembers their first gig well:

> It was for a colleague at Molins, Dennis Bristow, and it was held at Downley Village Hall. The best part was we never even had a microphone! Can you imagine that, a band with no microphone? But we managed and a good time was had by all, as they say.

From that moment on, the band developed a style that was popular amongst their friends and acquaintances and gradually they built up quite a following as a result. 'Most of our gigs were gained by word of mouth, as we never advertised ourselves, and soon we were booked up months in advance, so we must have been doing something right.' Most of the time the band played at clubs and sports clubs around the town and they did lots of weddings and parties. Pete continues:

> Dave Purdom used to live in the prefabs at Brooke Road with his Mum, until he was offered a job in Birmingham as a pathologist. I actually arranged for him to lodge at my Mum and Dad's house whilst he worked there, but he always managed to get back to Risborough for the gigs at the weekends. Then one day we were due to play at Molins Clubhouse in Mill Lane, Monks Risborough, and the rest of us turned up for the gig okay, but there was no sign of Dave. There was no phone at Molins at that time so I walked up to the phone box near the Nag's Head pub on the Aylesbury Road and phoned my Dad and asked him what time Dave had left for Risborough? With that I heard Dad shout, 'DAVE!' He was still in my Mum and Dad's watching telly and hadn't even left! He had forgotten to put the gig in his diary and didn't realise we had one that week. So, I went back to Molins and told the others that Dave wasn't coming. Luckily we managed to get through the gig without him and with the help of an old mate from Molins, Stan Gale, who muddled through on piano for us. Mind you, we probably only got away with it because we were playing the gig for all our other mates from Molins.

Another story Pete tells is of the night at the British Legion when the band almost made their last performance… ever!

> We were playing upstairs in the Legion, in the mid-1970s it was, stomping our way through a group of numbers, when I felt a slight vibration on my lips from the microphone. I immediately signalled to Dave Farris on drums to cut after this song so I could check the gear. But to my

amazement he started another number with a 'one, two, three, four' and we were into 'The Green Green Grass of Home'! I nearly had a fit and just to be safe I held the mike well away from my mouth, but yes, you've guessed it, halfway through the song, without any warning, BANG! The shock went right down my throat, knocking me backwards straight through the drums and drummer, both of us hitting the wall, drums and cymbals everywhere! It not only blew a fuse in the Legion but I think it put half of Risborough into darkness. It knocked me for six and I was all for finishing there and then, for good! But unbelievably the gig continued for another two hours, still with no power and just some candlelight. We carried on with just piano, sax and a drum and brushes and it turned out to be one of the best sing-song's Risborough has ever seen. I don't know how long it took for the power to come back on, it certainly wasn't that night, and I think the only thing that saved me was the rubber soles on my shoes. Let's just say they nearly came to see me in the shade of that old oak tree!

After about a year Dave Purdom left the band and it then went to five members when Ted Saunders and Mike Goodearl joined:

Ted was a few years older than us but he had a brilliant Hammond organ which he used to cart around for the gigs. Mick was in bands on and off for most of his life and was an excellent musician. We later had Dave Janes, Geoff Roman and finally Mick Brooks at various times, but always we stayed as a five-piece band. We tried hard to keep up with the songs of the day

The Dave Peterson Five.

and through the '60s, '70s and '80s we would take note of all the new stuff coming out on the radio. If someone like The Beatles or Tom Jones, for instance, brought out a new song, we would try and incorporate it into our shows as soon as possible. It seemed to go down well with our audiences.

Another little known fact about one of Risborough's best ever bands was that Harold Mitchell was their roadie. Fellow Molins man Harold deserves a chapter in this book all to himself, such was his character, and there are a thousand and one stories about the man who co-founded Risborough Tenants FC. In fact, as it turns out, he used to ferry the footballers to the away games on a Saturday afternoon and then come home and go straight out again to ferry The Dave Peterson Five to their latest gig. His old Bedford twelve-seater van worked overtime! Pete recalls:

It was not unusual for Harold to come off a night-shift at Molins on the Saturday morning, spend all morning working on the Tenants pitch, take the lads to football in the afternoon and then pick us up and take us to our gig that night. He would drive us all the way to somewhere like Buckingham for instance, drop us off, and then go home for a few hours sleep, before coming back for us when the gig finished! Harold was a one-off that's for sure.

There will be more about Harold later...

As the band's popularity grew, the area that they played in grew too. Pete recalls:

We had a circle of gigs that we played regularly, but gradually that circle grew a bit wider. We played at places like Gomme's in Wycombe, the Green Shield Stamp place, Flackwell Heath FC, Hazells, Rivets, Thame United Social Club and clubs at Booker and Cressex. We always came back to Risborough regularly though, and always played the Poppy Day Dance at the Legion and other special occasions in the town. And wherever we played we always put the bar takings up as we used to drink a fair bit ourselves! In between songs of course!

The band continued to entertain the Risborough and district public for twenty years until in the early 1980s, they decided that enough was enough. Pete remembers:

When we decided to pack up we had bookings for three years ahead but we were beginning to wonder where it was all going to end. I kept thinking to myself if it was right for this forty-three-year-old bloke to still be prancing about a stage belting out pop songs? In the end we all sat down one night, over a pint, and decided that we would call it a day. In fact we decided that we would give it one more year. And do you know, that year was one of the best we ever had. Whether it was because we knew we were finishing and we all relaxed more I'm not sure, but that year was brilliant.

Pete and his wife Jean have now been married for over fifty years and they still live in the same house in Westmead. 'I always remember the year we were married,' says Pete, 'It is etched on the heart – it was 1957, the year Aston Villa won the FA Cup!' That passion for his beloved Aston Villa reveals the other part of Pete's contribution to Risborough life, his

Eddie Prince and the Creole Combo.

The Cavaliers.

dedication to boy's football in the town. There will be more of that in our chapter about Risborough sport.

But before we leave the music scene, we need to mention some of the other top bands that Risborough has had to offer in those years gone by. The Vic Good Band often appeared in the town, as did short-lived bands like The Risborough Shindigs, a four-piece band that included Ted Haynes and Billy McCorkell Senior amongst their members. They actually recorded a single called 'Alone' which was written by Billy in ten minutes in his kitchen. The record came out at the same time as 'Michelle', by The Beatles. Sadly, the Risborough record did not quite sell as many copies but on the 'B' side was a version of 'Speedy Gonzalez' and The Beatles could not compete with that. At least one copy of The Risborough Shindig's record is known to still exist to this day!

Another band that appeared in many local gigs was The Creole Combo. In that band you had Dave Simmons, Trevor Stott, Mick Cotter and Spikey Hubbard. Later on, another singer came in called Eddie Prince, and in fact the band was later called Eddie Prince and the Creole Combo. Pete Boland remembers Eddie as a forerunner of Shakin' Stevens!

In the early 1960s, at a time when groups were forming in almost every town in England, several Risborough lads formed The Blobbs, which included Roger (Gutty) Ridgeway on bass and Paul Wightman on drums with Mick Thompson and Mike Avery. Later Paul went on to have some success with a band called The Cavaliers, which also included Roger Messer, James Finlay, Mike Avery and later, Les Payne, Brian Wallace and Dave Bone. Les then broke away to form a band called Chameleon, with Mick Evans, Vaughan Wallis and Alan Goodchild. Later, Tom Goodearl and Bob Pearce joined Chameleon and the group actually came very close to real success, as did former Courtmoor resident, Les Payne. His

Chameleon.

later band, Mainland, performed as the support act on a nationwide Leo Sayer tour in 1979. You can still see Les performing today, in person, or on YouTube.

There was another local musician who made it to the big time though. Nigel Harrison was born in Stockport, in Cheshire, but he was brought up and went to school in Princes Risborough. In fact, Mike Goodearl taught him much of what he learned. Nigel played bass for a local band called Farm before going on to fame and fortune by joining Blondie in 1977. He even wrote their 1982 single 'War Child', which spent four weeks in the charts and reached number thirty-nine. Harrison is now bass player for a group called The Grabs. Les Payne remembers the time when he lived at Courtmoor in Mill Lane when Nigel would come to his house for a jamming session.

And did you also know that once upon a time Genesis played a gig in the British Legion? They were late replacements for a band called Writing on the Wall and Genesis already had in their ranks at the time Phil Collins, Mike Rutherford and Peter Gabriel. It was one of their claims to fame that Risborough band Chameleon played on the same bill that night, back in October 1970. Were you there one wonders?

Apart from Genesis and Nigel Harrison, the only one of those names still regularly playing live is Les Payne, still often seen gigging in and around Risborough. Nowadays of course, television shows like *The X Factor* and *Britain's Got Talent* look for the big stars of tomorrow, but so far there has not been a Princes Risborough act discovered. However, the musical talent is still in the town, and you only have to visit the local schools to find that out.

Les Payne at Courtmoor.

Chapter Five

The Long Arm of the Law

Princes Risborough was a pretty easy place to police in the 1940s and '50s. The town was still quite small and there were few nasty outside influences in those days. So, being a policeman in the town was a fairly relaxed job and the 'bobby on the beat' was a comforting sight for the local inhabitants.

Names like Frank Dean, Jim Purdy and a few others held the post, but one man stands head and shoulders above all others when it comes to remembering ex-Risborough bobbies. Dave Allworth was actually born in Dorrington in Lincolnshire in 1937 and was the son of a former Navy man. His Dad was eventually seconded to the special services in the RAF, stationed at RAF Cranwell. Later he was to transfer to RAF Halton when Dave was fourteen years old, and this move was to determine the youngster's future.

Dave remembered the first time he considered becoming a policeman:

When I was about ten years old I used to sit outside the front of my house and collect car numbers, as small boys did, and one day the local bobby came by on his bike and stopped to have a chat. He was particularly interested in looking at my car numbers, and I later realised that he was checking to see if there was anyone moving around that had excess petrol during those ration conscious days. So, innocently, I was aiding and abetting the police even then!

After the family moved to Halton, Dave spotted an advert in the press, looking for people to apply to join the Metropolitan Police Cadets:

I applied and lo and behold I was accepted and began my basic training. But at the time National Service was compulsory and I ended up doing my stint in the RAF. Even then, as someone with a little police experience, they put me with the RAF Police Unit. My Dad thought it would all be a good experience for me, as he seemed to think I would have a chance to see the world. Alas, I ended up in Bedfordshire and Cannock Chase and never even saw the sea!

On his release from National Service, Dave tried to rejoin the Metropolitan Police as he felt his opportunities would be greater there. But he was told that there was at least a nine-month wait for admission:

> When you are a nineteen- or twenty-year-old, nine months is a long time, and I was impatient and couldn't be doing with all that waiting around. Then one day I was out on my motorbike and found myself in Kingsbury Square in Aylesbury. When you have had some involvement as a policeman you always end up speaking to other police officers, and that day one ambled past me and I started chatting to him. As I'm speaking to this chap his sergeant arrived and, to cut a long story short, the next thing I know I'm in Walton Street Police Station talking about joining the Bucks Constabulary! The following Tuesday I went back there and signed up and completed my further training with them.

On reflection Dave realises that he probably should have waited and joined the Metropolitan Police. 'Promotion and advancement would have been a lot easier there and policing out in the sticks gave little chance of promotion. But the Met's loss was to be Risborough's gain,' says Dave with a twinkle in his eye.

He was first posted to High Wycombe and it was whilst there that he met his future wife Ann:

> Asking Ann to marry me was definitely the best move I ever made, but the start to our married life was not easy as soon afterwards I was posted to Winslow, where we were given a tiny flat above the local Police Station. It was very cramped to say the least, and if her Mum came to visit, the flat was so small I had to sleep in one of the cells!

Dave stayed at Winslow for a while but then came the news that Ann was expecting a baby!

> That was a bit of a shock because there was no way that we could have three of us sharing that tiny flat in Winslow. But, as luck would have it, I managed to wangle a transfer to Princes Risborough and we moved in to a much bigger house in New Road. That was in 1958 and my new patch had a population of around 5,000 at the time. Little did I know then that for the next fifty years I would become part of that community.

When Dave first arrived in Princes Risborough, the new Co-op was being built at the top end of the High Street. He recalls:

> It was one of my first patrols on a night shift that I ever did and as I was passing the hoarding covering the new building site, I heard a suspicious noise so I went to investigate. I clambered into the site and the next thing I knew I was up to my ankles in wet cement! Somewhere in the foundations of that building you could probably still see the footprint of my TUF boot!

As the years went on Dave certainly forged a reputation as a 'no-nonsense copper' but he also won the respect of most of the town's population. He had a simple philosophy about policing. If you kept out of trouble he wouldn't bother you, but woe betide anyone who stepped out of line. He didn't earn the nickname 'Bookie' for nothing! But the important respect he held was in keeping the crime in the town in check and many people have said to us in our research for this book that seeing 'Bookie' coming up the road used to put the fear of God in them! He had an uncanny knack of knowing where all the teenagers hung out, and always had his finger on the pulse and ear to the ground. It was a sixth sense to him.

Eunice Clifford remembers one incident as she and her husband Colin drove back along the Wycombe Road after a night out.

We looked in the mirror and thought, oh no, there's a police car following us! We were a little worried because we had had a few drinks that night. Anyway we drove home and as we pulled into the drive of our house in Crossfield Road, the police car pulled up behind us. It was Bookie! As we stepped out a voice said, 'Blimey it's Colin and Eunice, I didn't know you lived here?' (We had just recently moved in). 'Tell you what Colin,' continued Dave, 'you had better

Dave 'Bookie' Allworth.

get that rear light fixed before someone pulls you over!' And with that we went indoors and made him a cup of tea! And that was the sort of copper Dave was!

One incident Dave remembers well also highlights the impact he had:

I was in the Police Station along the Wycombe Road when I received a call to say that there had been an incident at the Carlton Cinema. Apparently one of the local hard cases, who was a bit of a Teddy Boy and known to me, had been sat downstairs in the cinema just below the edge of the balcony. Up above, in the balcony seats, were four or five of his arch enemies. They saw him sat there and decided to buy some ice cream, melt it on the radiators and then promptly pour it all over his Teddy Boy outfit. Well, you can imagine how annoyed our friend was. He went berserk, climbed up to the balcony seats and then threw three of the lads over the top! The ambulance was also called, as there were some nasty injuries. I set off to answer my callout, knowing full well who the Teddy Boy was and knowing that I was heading for a confrontation. At the bottom of Clifford Road I bumped into an off-duty colleague and decided to take him with me. He was an ex-stoker and as tough as old boots. When we reached the cinema there was this Teddy Boy at the top of the steps looking as though he had spent too long in Trafalgar Square amongst the pigeons! As my colleague approached he was kicked in the chest. With that we had some sorting out to do and my colleague subdued the lad round the side of the cinema. I tried to sort out inside and eventually everything calmed down. The stoker dealt with the Teddy Boy, but later it was found that none of the lads upstairs would press charges against him. Anyway to cut another long story short, our friend never gave us any more trouble after that, and in fact went on to help me in a number of petty crimes in the town, not least in identifying the person who once stole one of the hands off the Market Square clock!

Many residents never got to know the other, lighter side of the tough copper from Lincolnshire. Co-author Mike Payne remembers playing football with him for a team called Westmead, run by Tom Gilmour:

Dave was always a tough performer on the football field, a centre-half stopper in the old-fashioned mould. If it moved he usually kicked it. But he did laugh once when we were playing a match at Beaconsfield against a team of Ghurkhas. Most of them came on to the pitch barefoot! Dave looked at me and said, 'I'm going to enjoy this!' Although as it turned out, they were so quick he couldn't get near them!

Dave also remembered a funny incident that happened at the barber's shop:

I needed a haircut and went to the town and looked at the prices at Nicholl's but on my copper's pay I felt it was a bit steep, so I took the cheaper option and went to Roy Gilbert's place opposite. Anyway, I was sat in the chair chatting to Roy, as you do, and afterwards paid him, and went home. When I got home Ann said to me, 'What's happened to your hair?' When I looked in the mirror I noticed that because we were talking so much, Roy had only done half my head! The annoying thing was, when I went back down the town Roy had closed his shop and I had to go to Mr Nicholls after all to get it tidied up!

Westmead FC. Dave Allworth is
second from right, back row.

Contrary to popular belief, there was also a little-known softer side to Dave's nature as
well, as co-author Angela Payne remembers:

> When my Dad [Wally Burton, the gent's hairdresser] died suddenly in his sleep in 1988, Dave
> Allworth was the policeman on duty who had to attend the sudden death. Dave often used
> to pop in to my Dad's shop and have a chat, and when he realised it was Dad who had died,
> he broke his heart. I shall never forget seeing him go outside and wipe the tears from his eyes.

So, there was no doubt that over the years that Dave earned a great deal of respect from
everyone in the town, and he was to eventually put in thirty years' service with the force.
He later worked for the council and indeed, he eventually became a Princes Risborough
Councillor, and later Chairman of the Town Council. 'As with my life as a policeman, I did
tend to upset a few people, but I like to think I gave my all for the town and managed to
get a few things done.'

There are not too many people who would argue with that.

Author's Note: Sadly, as we were preparing this book, and shortly before Christmas 2008,
we heard the tragic news that Dave Allworth had died. He had been ill for some time and
we were so lucky to have had the chance to speak to him about his life and career. When
we arrived at his house that late summer's afternoon, Dave was feeling a bit down, but by
the time we left, and he had had the chance to recount some of those great stories about
his life, the old familiar Dave Allworth sparkle reappeared in his eyes. We hope he enjoyed
our visit as much as we did. Thank you, Dave.

Chapter Six

Family Life and the Age of Innocence

Quite a number of large families grew up in Princes Risborough during the 1950s. Those families had little by way of possessions, but what they did have in abundance was a really happy and healthy outlook on life, and lots and lots of fun. The Attridge clan was a typical example of one such family.

There were seven of them in all: Dad (Richard) and Mum (Sue), and then their children, Joyce, Gillian, Shelagh, Roland and Jeremy. Richard and Sue first came to Risborough from their native Ireland, just after the war when Richard found work here. They first lived in Summerleys Road and then Berryfield Road before settling into their house in Ash Road. When the children began arriving in the early 1950s, the needs of the family grew and Richard certainly made full use of his garden, as well as an allotment, throughout his life. It was a necessity by the end of the decade and helped feed his family. Daughter Gill recalls:

> We grew everything in our garden from tomatoes, lettuce and other salad items to potatoes, cabbages, brussel sprouts and a huge variety of other vegetables. There was little need for Mum to buy hardly anything from the shops as we had most of what we needed on our own doorstep. We also had all the varieties of fruit too; strawberries, raspberries, gooseberries and blackcurrants, etc., so puddings were taken care of too. Mind you there was a lot of hard work in preparing this feast and we hardly saw our Dad at times. He worked nights at Molins for thirty-six years and any spare time he had he would be planting up the garden, or his allotment along the Longwick Road situated next to the Cheverton & Laidler factory. But all of his hard work really paid off and we all grew up eating lots of healthy food.

Shelagh recalls how, after the children were all married themselves, her Mum would frown if she knew the girls had gone out on shopping trips with friends and were not there to make their husbands a meal when they got in from work. She recalls:

> It was difficult for Mum to understand because no matter what time of night or day Dad got home from his shift work, Mum would have a hot dinner put in front of him. Even allowing

Molins Christmas party.

for the family's low income, we always had good wholesome meals during the week, including casseroles in every variation you could think of, and a roast dinner on Sundays.

Life in the house was hectic to say the least, but always exciting and as the children all began to grow, their days were very busy and full of fun. Joyce remembers:

We shared our toys and clothes and, especially in the summer, we played outside all day from dawn to dusk. Mum and Dad knew that we were safe, although some of the pranks we got up to in those days would break all of today's ridiculous health and safety rules! We used to play one great game with our neighbours, another large family, the Burtons, in Beech Road. We would wait for their Mum and Dad to go out, and then take a mattress off one of the beds upstairs and drag it around the front of the house. We would then climb out of the upstairs front bedroom window to the flat roof and then take great delight in jumping on to the mattress. We then ran upstairs and did it again and again! Only when our 'lookout' spotted their Mum coming home did we drag the mattress back upstairs as fast as our little arms and legs could manage.

'Great fun and we were only twenty-six at the time!' joked Roland. 'And then,' continued Joyce, 'we also used to climb out the bathroom window on to the back flat roof where we would roller skate! Again, health and safety out of the window, literally!'

The Attridge children.

Ready to play on the
green.

Making their own fun was a way of life for children of that era. And of course, people rarely left the estate they lived on. Most of the homes were council properties and the same people lived in them for years. It meant that all the families grew up together, went to school together and shared their lives together, as in the main neighbours remained unchanged throughout their childhood and beyond. It also meant that everyone knew everyone else too.

All the Attridges remember the times when a whole gang of children would tramp up to the Whiteleaf Cross or the chalk pits, 'We would spend all day making a "camp", eat a picnic from stuff we took from the pantry, play games and generally have a great time,' says Gill, 'And one day I remember going to Pyrtle Springs, one of our favourite haunts, taking with us some lemonade powder and cups. We would dip our cups into the water of the spring, add the lemonade powder and then tuck into our homemade drink! Delicious.'

Occasionally there were complaints from the neighbours, usually because of the noise the children made, but there was none of the maliciousness of today's world. Shelagh recalls:

We would often play rounders on the green for hours and hours, but every now and then the ball would fly off into one of the gardens. Some people took exception and kept the ball, which annoyed us. But we always respected our elders, something Mum and Dad drilled into us, and we would just go indoors and find another ball. You still had grumpy neighbours in those days, but it was part of life and we never knowingly damaged their property. It was called respect.

Joyce also remembers another area that they all loved playing in. 'When we were children there were no houses where Bell Lane is now, it was just waste land where we loved to play. On that piece of land there were some chicken coops and we used to use them as camps. They were our original Wendy houses!'

Special days of the year were also fondly remembered, with Guy Fawkes' night a particular favourite. Gill recalls:

I remember one year we arranged for the dustbin men to unload some of the rubbish from their lorry into our garden. They asked why we wanted it. 'For our bonfire', came the reply! But our Dad went spare when he saw all this pile of rubbish dumped at the end of his precious garden. Mind you, our bonfire was pretty spectacular that year! Another memory is of our neighbour, Mrs Burton, supplying the jacket potatoes. Only trouble was, she started cooking them from early in the morning of firework night and by the time we came to eat them they were like rocks!

The family all had very fond memories of the shops in the town. Gill remembers the smells of Mr Redman's grocery store in Bell Street, 'And trying to find something still in date on the shelves!' Roland distinctly recalls buying Jamboree Bags at Robin Ball's sweet shop:

We used to go in after Sunday school. Mum and Dad gave us sixpence for Sunday school and thruppence to spend on sweets, or was it the other way round? Mum always bought our plimsolls in Leslie Herman's and I also remember doing a paper round for a few weeks in Adcocks & Percivals. Mr Adcock tried to persuade me to do a Sunday round and offered me an extra 15p per week to do it. I turned him down and gave up the other round shortly afterwards.

Like everyone else we have spoken to during our research for this book the Attridge family all remember Adcocks with affection. 'Papers were on the left, food on the right and toys at the back of the shop,' says Gill. 'Upstairs was the prams and bikes and a train set was laid out for all the children to see. I also remember a chap named Dan Ashford who drove the Adcocks van around the town.'

The family occasionally had a break from Risborough and enjoyed some good holidays together. Joyce recalls one of their favourite places:

> We always looked forward to our holidays and we had several lovely stays at Bracklesham Bay in Sussex. I also remember one year going to Clacton on the train from Risborough. My goodness! That was a long trip. We went in to London, lugged our heavy cases across the capital, before changing trains to head for Clacton. One year Dad actually won a holiday for two in Spain on one of those Spastic Society competitions that a collector used to deliver around the doors. Dad was crestfallen, 'But I've got five kids!' he protested. Anyway, in the end the prize was amended to a holiday for the whole family at Camber Sands!

Sadly, the Attridge family lost their Mum, Sue, at Christmas 2008, but her lovely dry Irish humour lives on through the memories of her children. At Sue's funeral, Shelagh read a lovely tribute to her Mum that she had written, and one part we would like to reproduce here. It is something we are sure many families will identify with. Shelagh said:

> Mum would worry what the neighbours thought if the grass was too long or the hedge too high, but she would not blink an eye at the thought of embarrassing us as teenagers on holiday, by sitting on the beach in her bra, because 'nobody knew her there' and 'they could look all they wanted!' She even repeated the performance years later, horrifying some of her grandchildren on a day trip to Margate. It was unexpectedly hot and there were cries of, 'Oh no! Look at Nanny!' Mum was sat in her deckchair, in her bra, with an added bonus this time of the T-shirt she had just removed being used as a sunhat!

It was an expensive business bringing up five children and sometimes the budget had to be stretched a bit. For instance, many of the clothes the children wore tended to be handed down and Shelagh recalls that in her case, most of her clothes were third hand-me-downs! And Roland jokes, 'For the first five years of my life I was dressed as a girl, and I'm still trying to get over it!'

All in all though, the children had an idyllic childhood. Life was so much simpler for children of the '50s. You could play safely in the road because there were few cars about, all of their games were imaginative and fun, they rarely watched television and they took advantage of the wonderful natural surroundings that Risborough had to offer. They were also able to share their lives with lots of other children of their own age. Now, all those Attridge children have married and have children of their own, but now and again they let their kids know just what an adventurous childhood they all had. Happy days.

Chapter Seven

Mysteries of the Lab Revealed

There are still quite a few people who live in Princes Risborough whose parents, grandparents and even great-grandparents also lived in the town. One such person is Sylvia Wynands whose great-grandparents on her mother's side, whose surname was Chowns, came from Risborough. But it was strange how people then came in to the town from outside and somehow found themselves joining these families. It happened to Sylvia's family twice:

> My father, Horace Webster, was from Northamptonshire. He was a builder and during the mid-1920s he heard about some work going in a Buckinghamshire town called Princes Risborough, so he thought he would try his luck. As soon as he got here he looked for digs and someone told him that there was a Mrs Ada Brooks who took in lodgers. That was my Grandmother, and it was whilst he was living there that he met my mother.

The work that Mr Webster found was the building of a new laboratory in Summerleys Road, a laboratory that was being set up to study the economical use of various timbers. It was the birth of the Forest Products Research Laboratory, opened in June 1927.
Sylvia recalls:

> Some of my early memories of my Dad was seeing him in his garden. He grew everything in it and he also kept chickens too. He was always working on his garden, planting it up or harvesting all the crops he grew. They never had to buy much food from the shops, but I can also still see to this day the fish man coming round to the house, and Mum and Dad would buy sprats from his van. They certainly made a tasty meal.

Ironically, the laboratory would again feature heavily in Sylvia's life in the 1950s as for the second time an 'outsider' came to town and joined her family:

> Well, actually, it was where I met my husband Ron. Ron, who originally came from Stoke Newington, had been an evacuee from London at the start of the Blitz when he was eventually

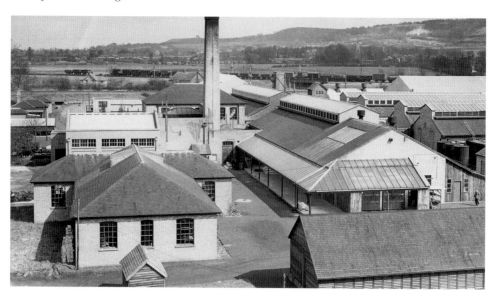

The Forest Products Research Laboratory.

sent to live in High Wycombe. After his schooling and National Service was over he was offered a job at the Lab, and because I also worked there, in the drawing office, we met and he later asked me out. We were later married in 1957 and have just celebrated over fifty years of marriage.

Ron remembers, 'There were lots of marriages between the staff at the Lab and there must have been something like twenty couples who married after meeting there.' That is something that the Lab shares with some of the other leading employers in the town, as there were also many marriages recorded between staff at Molins, staff at Cheverton & Laidler's and staff at the other big employers in the town.

The Timberlab, as it was to be known, had a long and interesting history, but to the people of the town it also held many mysteries, and to some extent there was an air of suspicion about the place. For a start it was often falsely believed that it was a Ministry of Defence establishment. Ron explains:

That was not true, but I can understand where the confusion came from. It was originally set up after the First World War. After that war ended, the country, and the world in general, was very short of timber. So it was decided to make a study of all the different types of trees that were available at home and in the Empire, as it was then, looking also at the suitability of certain woods and what they could be best used for. It was a very specialist field of expertise and we even had our own siding from the station so that the logs could be shipped in direct to us from abroad. Sylvia's father later got a job at the site and was put in charge of taking delivery of all the timber. We also had a special section of entomology, which studied the effects beetles and bugs had on the wood. The building that that department was housed in is the only part of the original lab buildings still standing on the site today. Sadly, all the other buildings housing the other ten research sections have now gone.

It was during the Second World War that the MOD connection came about, although it had nothing to do with the Lab. Ron continues:

> What happened was that when the Blitz began in earnest, a unit was set up by the Ministry of Home Security to study the economic effects of various bombing strategies, to see what information could be obtained from it. Because of the fierce bombing in London it was decided to set up the unit on a site in the country and the site of the Forest Products Research Laboratory was chosen. There was plenty of room on the site and some old World War One huts were hastily erected to hold the 200 or so people that came to work there. Funnily enough you may remember the famous BBC broadcaster, Dr Jacob Bronowski, who was an expert in Mathematics and Biology and who later became famous as the presenter of the acclaimed BBC series called *The Ascent of Man*. He actually worked for the ministry at their Risborough site when he was a young man. The operation was certainly very security conscious, and their part of the site was enclosed by a high fence. There was also their own fully armed Army sentries on duty at all times. So that is why the MOD theory was so prevalent in the town.

There was another connection to the Lab from the government during the war too. After some problems were encountered with the Anderson shelter during air raids, moves were made to design other shelters. One of these was the Morrison shelter, named after Home Secretary Herbert Morrison, and it was rumoured that Winston Churchill sketched the original idea on an old envelope and handed it to Mr Morrison saying, 'That is what you want.' As the designers worked on the project they enlisted the help of the Forest Products Research Laboratory at Princes Risborough and a prototype shelter was built in their workshops. It was later taken to No. 10 Downing Street and shown to the Prime Minister on New Year's Day 1941. Another prototype was also taken to No. 10 and in the end, Churchill approved both designs and by the end of January 1941, both types had been fully tested at Risborough and both were manufactured in great quantities so that the public could then make their preferred choice.

It was also fair to say that there was also a little bit of resentment from the locals towards the Lab as they very rarely took on local workers. But the reason for that was because about eighty or ninety of the 130-strong workforce came there straight from university, or from another similar laboratory in Farnborough. The work was so specialised that you needed to be a fully qualified scientist or engineer to do most of the work on the site.

Living in Princes Risborough during the war years brings back vivid memories for Sylvia, but another mystery she is struggling to clear up is finding anyone who can remember a fish and chip shop in Station Road during the 1930s. 'It was run by two women for quite a few years but no matter how I try I cannot find any photographic evidence of it existing. It was definitely there, as other people remember it, but I would love to find a photo of that shop.'

Sylvia remembers the unexploded bomb that was found in Clifford Road behind the Bell Street School:

> We were all given time off school whilst Army bomb disposal experts made it safe, so it was very exciting! Of course we never realised quite how dangerous it all was. We really

didn't see too much of the war in Risborough to be honest, but I do recall one incident that actually made us smile. It was not unusual for people to come from the city and be billeted in Risborough. We had many people coming and going, staying with us at our Wycombe Road house, and one young lad staying with us leapt out of bed when he heard the air-raid siren and hid under the stairs. 'Always did that in Ramsgate,' he said. Of course that is what he had been used to doing at home, and I must admit that my brother Derek and I thought it a wonderful idea to get up after being put to bed, to go under the stairs, although Mother told us to 'sit good, and not think we could play'. The novelty soon wore off. And when the air-raid siren went off, my father, if on fire watch, had to get on his bike and rush to protect the Lab, leaving us to look after ourselves.

Sylvia also recalls the importance of the railway line into Risborough in those dark days of war:

The height of the Blitz was an horrendous time for Londoners and quite often we would hear a knock on our door late at night, and answer it to find exhausted and frightened people who had come out of London by train just to escape the awful bombing and to try and get at least one full night's sleep. They got off the train and made for the nearest houses just to find some relief from it all. One night a lady knocked on the door with two little girls. She was told we would help them. My mother rushed about with blankets making up beds, and then the next morning they would return to London. Of course, the country was all pulling together at that time so there was no thought of turning anyone away, and we would happily put them up for the night. Then, the next morning they would go back to London on the train to do their day's work. It must have been a terrible time for them all.

But there was still some fun to be had by the locals and on Saturday nights the Walsingham Hall was a hotbed of entertainment. Sylvia recalls:

There would be a dance most weeks and there used to be a band called The Black Aces who would play the music and everyone would dance the night away. Around about ten o'clock, the Buckingham Arms would empty out and some of the lads would come over to the dance, sometimes the worse for wear! I remember Daisy Simmons, née Saw, used to serve teas from the little room at the back of the hall. And did you know that a room at the back of the Walsingham Hall, behind the stage, was used as a lending library two evenings a week, manned by staff from the Lab? I remember the Carlton Cinema being built next to Bell Street School. Coaches used to bus in people from all the outlying villages just so they could go to the pictures. The queue on a Saturday night sometimes stretched right along Bell Street. And one other memory I have as regards entertainment was the old British School building at the end of Station Road, on the junction of Wycombe Road. They turned that into a roller skating rink at times and that used to be great fun. As for going to Wycombe or Aylesbury, well, that would be a big adventure in those days, although later I did go to school in Wycombe, so the travel became a bit more accepted by me at that time.

After the war it was quite hard to readjust to peacetime again, as Ron observed:

Like everywhere else in the country, lads were coming back from war, some from POW camps and often with bad experiences, so it was hard for everyone. Then in the 1950s National Service came in and the lads were coming and going from the Lab, just as in every other walk of life. I remember one of those lads, Tim Titmus, had come from a Japanese POW camp. When he worked at the Lab he started a drama group called the 101 Players. The reason he chose that name was because the phone number of the Lab in those days was Risborough 101! Sylvia regularly appeared in the productions, and they were all really good. The one thing Tim couldn't get used to though was hearing the female voices. He had set up something similar in the prison camp and, of course, in those productions all the roles had to be played by men. Anyway we all survived the transition into normal life again and just moved on with our lives. I met and married Sylvia and we lived in Poppy Road, and over fifty years later we have our own personal reasons to thank the Forest Products Research Laboratory for setting up their base in Princes Risborough.

Ron later became a prominent member of the Risborough Parish Council, as it was then, and he gave many years loyal service to the community, as he still does. He has also had an active interest in sport:

I remember in the 1970s, we bought ourselves a football for £5 and set up a five-a-side team at the Lab. This gradually grew to several teams and we played inter-departmental games. Then we had the idea to hold a local five-a-side tournament, and for a few years the Timberlab five-a-sides was a regular part of the local football calendar. We held it on our grounds, marked out several pitches, built some goalposts, made our own trophies, and the crowds and teams flocked in. We also started an archery club at the Lab too and that developed into the district's top archery club, and the ladies of the Lab even had a cricket team. It was jokingly said that if you played cricket

A production from the 101 Players.

A St John's Ambulance day trip.

then you were guaranteed a job at the Lab, such was the enthusiasm for the game by the Assistant Director, STC Stillwell. There was certainly plenty of entertainment for the workforce and no excuse not to get involved.

Sylvia became an enthusiastic member of the Princes Risborough St John's Ambulance Brigade, helping lots of youngsters through their first-aid courses. 'I always looked forward to Kimble Races, as we were always put on duty there, and there was always plenty of cuts, bruises and breaks to attend to when the jockeys came off their horses!' And Sylvia wanted one other memory to be recorded in their story:

> Before the war I remember vividly my Dad would look out of the window and say, 'There goes Amy Johnson, riding her horse.' Amy, of course, was the pioneering aeroplane pilot who achieved many flying records and in 1930 became the first woman to fly solo to Australia. She lived in a house down the lane off Church Square, and she actually used to ride past our house and then turn up the Icknield Way. We also used to see the famous writer and author, Denise Robins, who also lived in Risborough.

It was Sylvia and Ron whose suggestion it was to have a Blue Plaque put on Amy Johnson's old house to commemorate the feats of a remarkable woman.

Chapter Eight

Risborough Through and Through

Just like in other parts of England there are many characters in the town of Princes Risborough, and one of those personalities knows more than most about the changes seen in the town over the last sixty years or more. Dennis Eggleton is a loyal and hard-working resident who contributed so much to the community throughout his working life. He has been married to his lovely wife, Angela, for forty-five years now, and they both take great delight in remembering their lives together and reflecting on the changes they have seen.

Dennis's family began a bakery business back in the mid-nineteenth century in Monks Risborough, called Eggleton's Bakery, and from the moment he was born he was destined to one day take on the duties his parents, grandparents, great-grandparents and great-great-grandparents had continued for over 100 years. For all of that time his family had baked bread for the villages of Monks Risborough and Princes Risborough, and all the outlying villages on the Aylesbury side. Dennis recalls:

> We are not sure of the actual year that it all started, but certainly it does go back at least four generations. I certainly remember my Grandad's involvement. A while back we were visiting some friends and they were showing me a book, about railways funnily enough, and we made a remarkable discovery. Towards the back of the book we came across this amazing picture of a character in a white overall preparing a horse and cart for deliveries. The caption said it was a 'Mr Smith, the farrier', but on closer inspection I realised that it was my grandfather getting the horse ready for the bread deliveries! That was later to be confirmed by an Aunt of mine who recognised him too. I had never seen that photograph before, so it was a real find, and I have since obtained a copy from the book publishers, having also put them right over their caption.

That picture was dated 1903 and Dennis's father, Walter Eggleton, was five years old at the time. Thirteen years later his Dad joined the Army and served in the First World War. Then after his demob, he was to join the family business and he eventually took over from his father, also named Walter. Dennis continues:

I remember Dad telling me that when he came out of the Army he had a chance to buy a thatched cottage in Burton Lane. It was the one with '1590' above the door, the date signifying the year it was built. Anyway the lady who was selling it, who lived in Kimble, wanted £100 for it. Now that was a lot of money in those days, but Dad felt it was a deal too good to miss. He went to the bank and managed to arrange the money. But when he went back with the cash to complete the deal with the lady, she changed her mind and wouldn't sell him the cottage. She later sold it to a complete stranger saying that if she had sold it to my Dad, it might have upset his brothers and sisters. Dad had two brothers and five sisters. But Dad was a bit annoyed with her as he missed out on what would have been a great deal.

You can still see that cottage today, and at one time Dr Gould from the Cross Keys Practice lived there.

The bakery, and a shop that went with it, was situated in Burton Lane, down the side of the old Nag's Head pub. Dennis continues:

My Dad continued to run the business for many years with the help of his brother, Arthur, and his sisters, who worked mainly on the door to door deliveries. Sometime in the 1920s though, they moved the bakery part of the business across the road from the shop. They needed extra room and some larger ovens were put in. The demand was growing fast and they made their deliveries with a horse and cart, loading up the bread and trotting off to villages like Kimble, Marsh, Longwick, Ellesborough and Butlers Cross. But then in 1928, Dad bought his first van. He was buying it off a chap from Thame, who one day drove it over to Dad. He showed Dad how to drive it and then went with him as far as Kimble to make sure he was okay with it. At Kimble they stopped and the chap said that Dad would be fine with it from there on. He got out and promptly set off to walk back to Thame, leaving my Dad to drive back to Risborough. And that was the only driving experience Dad had before taking ownership of his new van, Risborough to Kimble!

Eggleton's Bakery became very busy through those years. Bread was the staple food for everyone in those days, and it was difficult to keep up with the demand. All the surrounding villages and schools were kept supplied, and the firm also supplied Chequers, the country home of the Prime Minister. Dennis recalls:

We actually served eleven different Prime Ministers during our time supplying bread to Chequers. We also had lots of regular customers in the villages, who would come to the van and buy our bread. Large families would sometimes buy a dozen or more loaves in a day! Dad and his brother must have worked all hours.

The villages of Princes Risborough and Monks Risborough have always been quite separate communities over the years, probably more so then than now:

We did supply a few people with bread in Princes Risborough, but they had their own bakers and we did not compete with them. Instead we concentrated on building up our rounds in Monks and the outlying villages. Our customers became our friends and in those days we would go into their houses, as the doors were always open. Sometimes, if nobody was about, I

Eggleton's Bakery, at your service.

would look in their bread bin myself, decide what they wanted, leave their new bread and go. Everyone trusted each other.

When Dennis left school he began to learn the baking trade at a firm in Aylesbury called Pages. He had been picking up tips as a boy for years, but now he was beginning to learn the business for real. But at that time the country had Military National Service and Dennis had to do his bit. When his Army career finished in 1958 the family business was fully staffed, so for a while he worked for Simmons Bakery in Poppy Road. It wasn't until his Dad's brother, Arthur, was taken poorly that Dennis returned to the family bakery:

> From then until the business closed in 1965 I ran the bakery. My Dad retired but I had the help of other chaps over the years. One person I remember well was a chap called Harold Stone, who lived in Station Road. He was so hard-working and reliable, and he loved his job there. We would prepare the bread the night before, mixing the flour and yeast and then leaving it all overnight. Harold would come in at five o'clock in the morning and start the baking process. The bread would go in the ovens at about 7 a.m. and then we would have a bit of breakfast. About forty-five minutes later it would all be ready to load on to the vans before delivering to our customers.

The list of baking makes for interesting reading. Twenty-dozen doughnuts, fifteen-dozen currant buns, twenty-five-dozen sausage rolls, seventy lardy cakes, not to mention 2,000

Aylesbury Road with Eggleton's Bakery van coming out of Burton Lane.

loaves of bread! It was an amazing amount of work and it was all done in their small bakehouse in Burton Lane:

> We also made special cakes too, and even wedding cakes (I actually made the cake for our wedding in 1963), so we had little spare time. It was very hard work, although I remember once we had a rep come round trying to sell us a special grease gun for greasing the tins, which would make things a little easier for us. It cost about £40, which was a lot of money then. But we decided to buy one and when they delivered it I was out on the round and Harold took delivery. When I asked him for the invoice docket he said that there wasn't one as it was cash on delivery, and he had paid it. Harold hardly spent any money, he couldn't because he was always at work, but to have £40 in your back pocket was very unusual for anyone at the time. He never seemed to bother much about money. I remember I once found a couple of his unopened pay packets in a storeroom, and then on another day he queried the size of the pound notes. I explained that they were the new ones now but he said he had been worried about using them and had 200 of them at home! I eventually changed them in the bank for him. Harold was a great bloke though and one of the best workers we ever had.

As the years went on it became harder and harder to make the business profitable. Dennis remembers:

> The bread trade changed dramatically in the early 1960s with sliced bread the preference for most people as opposed to the whole loaves we supplied. We did eventually buy a slicing machine, but by that time the supermarkets were on the rise. We did close the Burton Lane shop and then opened a shop in Bell Street for a while, around 1961, but we also lost some of our staff to

people like Molins. Factory life gave them the whole weekend off whereas we had to work six days a week. I remember on Saturdays, I would be delivering all day and I would still be out until late on Saturday, going round with a basket. I would end up on the Ash Road estate and I recall finishing at Daisy Lawrence's house just as they were starting to watch *Dixon of Dock Green*!

It also became very expensive to buy the stock for the shop in Bell Street. Dennis continues:

The Brooke Bond tea rep used to come round every Wednesday and we would buy ¼lb packets of their tea for 1*s* 3*d* (6p) and we would sell them for 1*s* 6*d* (7½p). But then the supermarkets came in and places like Anthony Jackson's, on double Green Shield stamps day, would be selling that same packet of tea for 1*s* (5p). We couldn't compete with that. In fact, sometimes we used to buy the stuff from the supermarket ourselves and sell it in our shop! The Brooke Bond rep could never understand why we stopped ordering from him.

When the Wonderloaf factory opened in Wycombe and started delivering out into Risborough, it was the beginning of the end for Eggleton's Bakery and nearly 120 years of personal bakery service came to a sad end. 'We closed the business in 1965,' says Dennis, 'It was inevitable really because the larger supermarkets were taking over. Sadly, it is something that still happens today as the small businesses find it increasingly hard to compete. It takes a brave person to open a new retail business these days.'

Dennis then had to look ahead. He had met his future wife, Angela Phipps, in Hawkins café in the High Street, around 1958. Angela was born in Butlers Cross and had moved to Risborough, living in Eastfield Road, about five years before she met Dennis. They were eventually married in St Mary's Church in June 1963.

When you meet Dennis and Angela, you realise what a marvellous team they are. They say that behind every great man is a great woman, and Dennis would definitely agree with that. Angela gave Dennis great help behind the scenes in the later years of Eggleton's Bakery, helping with all the administration, and she has lots of fond memories of her own childhood too, and remembers things like the cherry cart coming down their street laden with lots of different cherries. She also has vivid memories of a fish and chip van visiting Butlers Cross. And after her family moved to Risborough, Angela worked in Adcocks on a Saturday morning whilst still at High School, and she and her sister loved to visit the Carlton Cinema to see the latest films.

It was a difficult decision for Dennis to close his business down, but it was also a tough decision deciding what he was going to do next. But with the support of Angela, he took a job with the Pearl Assurance and he was to remain with them until his retirement. Dennis recalls:

It was a very different career path for me, that's for sure, but in many ways the Pearl had the same personal touch that we tried to have in our bakery business. We would build up our round and become friends with our customers. The trust was built up too and I remember arranging small policies for the youngsters and when they grew up, they would then take out adult policies with me. So, it was still very much a family thing and I loved that personal contact, and I do miss that in today's world. Even after I retired I still carried on collecting

Dennis and Angela Eggleton's wedding day at St Mary's Church.

a few bits and pieces for the company, although by that time it had been taken over by an Australian firm and it was never the same.

We began this chapter introducing Dennis as a Risborough character, and Dennis himself remembers many others living in the town over the years. He says:

Oh, there used to be lots of chaps in the town who were real old-fashioned characters. There was Georgie Brown, who ran a fish stall at the market, Charlie Belgrove was another that springs to mind. Then there was Gilbert Young, the barber, who others have mentioned in this book, and two policemen, Cecil Smith and Frank Dean, who had their own unique way of policing the town. Frank Purcell was another, a farmer who once rode his horse into the George & Dragon for a bet! More recently, you had Robin Ball, a lovely man, and Robin's parents used to run the George at one time. Apparently they used to have a picture on the wall of the ladies loo of a Scotsman in a kilt. The kilt was a piece of cloth stuck to the picture, and it was attached to a bell in the bar. If one or two unsuspecting ladies lifted the kilt, the bell would ring! You can imagine the red faces as they came out of the loo and realised what everyone was laughing at! There was also Jack Kibble, the paraffin man, and many others too.

Dennis and Angela are still very active in the town and they still live in the house on the Aylesbury Road where Dennis was born. He grows all his own vegetables in his garden, which he tends lovingly, but more importantly he still makes his own bread occasionally. He says, 'I use Canadian flour, yeast and water, making sure the water is at the right temperature.' And he doesn't use a bread-making machine!

Once a Master Baker, always a Master Baker.

Chapter Nine

A True Princes Risborough Angel

When Barbara Saunders came to live in Princes Risborough in 1933, she could never have known just what a long-lasting legacy she was to leave to the town. Her Mum, Elizabeth, or Bet as she was known, was from Waddesdon and was one of ten children – nine girls and one boy. Her Dad, meanwhile, Albert Edward, known as Ted, was originally from London. When the family moved from Waddesdon to Risborough, Barbara spent her early years in No. 2 Longwick Road, going to school during the war in the old Church School opposite St Mary's Church.

Barbara remembers that school with much affection:

The hall that is still there today was in those days the whole school. It was divided up into three rooms and was the infants, junior and senior school when I was there. In fact I did all my schooling in that building. We did used to walk around to Bell Street, we called that the Council school, for cookery classes, but apart from that we stayed in Church Square. I remember Mr Coles, the Headmaster, and one or two of the teachers we had then. I really enjoyed those days, despite the fact that the war was on.

Like many others at the time, life went on very much as normal for people in Princes Risborough. But Barbara does have recollections of wartime incidents, like the occasion when a doodlebug flew over the house opposite. When the engine stopped, her Mum told her to get down and they dived for cover as the bomb did its damage. Barbara also recalls:

We often had convoys of soldiers coming through the town, occasionally stopping to use the shops or to do some training up Kop Hill or Pudding Hill. One day we got into trouble for being late for school because a Sherman tank was parked in the Market Square! When the teacher asked why we were late, we said that we couldn't get through because a Sherman tank was in the way! I also remember several women in Brooke Road were afraid to go into the van where they were to be fitted with gas masks! My Mum also took in some evacuees during the war and a few years ago, two of them came back to visit my Mum and it made the papers!

A class at St Mary's Church School.

But Barbara was to endure her worst time just at the end of the war. Her father, who had been invalided out of the RAF, had some serious health problems:

> Dad had kidney problems and when he was at home Mum would put him on a special diet, but when he was away with the RAF it was not possible for him to continue that diet, and as a result his health deteriorated. Sadly, Dad died just before the end of the war at just thirty-nine years of age. Our family doctor, Dr Edwards, was so kind to us at this time and he even helped my Mum arrange to move into a bungalow at Hawthorn Road shortly afterwards, because he feared our three-bedroom house would prove too big for her.

By this time Barbara was also about to leave school, so it was a traumatic time for her. But she started work in January 1945 for the local butcher, Ernie Morris, as a bookkeeper on 10s a week:

> I loved working with Mr Morris and his brothers and all the lads who worked in the shop. They were all really good to me. But a friend of mine later asked me if I would take on the same role at Jeffrey's the butchers, in Duke Street, and she offered me £1 10s 0d, so I went there. I stayed for two years, until I was seventeen years old, but then I decided on a completely different vocation. But I always loved living in Risborough and enjoyed going to the shops like Gillingwater's, Adcock's and dear Miss Lacey's shop that sold everything. She knew just where to put her hand on every single thing in that shop, even though it looked a jumbled mess when you went in! Rationing was still very strict but my Mum was a devil for sweets, I think she had a very sweet tooth, and I remember her sending my sister, Ann, up to Blue Kettle Jack's sweet shop at the bottom of Duke Street, to try and persuade him to let her have some of the next month's ration.

Barbara was looking towards having a career and the one thing she wanted to do more than anything else was to go into nursing. At that time, and for many years afterwards, getting into nursing following a secondary school education was not easy, as exam qualifications was a pre-requisite to becoming a nurse. Barbara recalls:

> One day my Mum was at a dance at the Walsingham Hall when she overheard somebody say that a matron at Stoke Mandeville was willing to take on a few girls from secondary education who were really keen to join the nursing profession. There were about six of us who applied and we all eventually made it through the training. I must admit that it was very tough and I struggled at times to keep up. Originally, because I was only seventeen years old, I had to join the Red Cross, as I couldn't move in to full nursing until I was eighteen. But I did do a variety of tasks and enjoyed some experience on the wards. Eventually I was able to train as a State Registered Nurse and by the time I finished at the hospital ten years later, I was a night sister.

The medical training was intense and very thorough. But it was not without its lighter side:

> We used to get the giggles at some of the lectures. There was one particular doctor, Dr Reynard his name was, and he looked a bit like a fox too! Anyway, he used to wear these crepe-soled shoes and he would squeak as he walked up and down giving his lecture. Of course this used to set off a couple of the girls into fits of giggles and that, in turn, set the rest of us off. 'What are you laughing at?' Dr Reynard would roar, but we couldn't answer for laughing!

Young Nurse Barbara (née Saunders) Wharton.

Barbara and her colleagues had to learn so much in their general nursing training. They would go to the Royal Bucks for their 'bones' training and would regularly work on a variety of wards in the Aylesbury hospitals. Barbara remembers:

> The night sisters used to ride their bikes up and down the long corridors at Stoke Mandeville to save their feet! But we did have some lovely patients during my time and I recall one particular patient who always said the same thing when I had to administer his dose of liquid paraffin. It was 1948 and all the chaps were ex-servicemen, and I can still see the man in his grey dressing gown to this day, holding out his glass and saying, 'In the mouth and round the gums, look out guts here it comes!' It used to make me laugh every time he said it.

In 1953 Barbara married John Wharton, a man she had known virtually all her life, as he had been a neighbour when she lived at Longwick Road. John had worked at Goodearl's before joining the forces, but after his demob he found a job on the railways and for many years he worked in the signal boxes on the Risborough to London line:

> John worked at Saunderton for a while but later came to Risborough station. At that time there were two signal boxes, with one a higher pay grade than the other. He worked at both of them until being made redundant in 1991 after forty years' service. We had two lovely children, Julie and Peter, and after first living in Woodfield Road we then moved to Merton Road.

Unfortunately for Barbara, she developed some health problems of her own, which meant that she could no longer carry out the physically demanding role of her hospital nursing. This, as it turned out, proved to be good fortune for Princes Risborough. Barbara recalls:

> Dr Edwards arrived in Risborough the same year as me and had known me since I was a small child, and once again he helped me, by offering me a job as the nurse at the Cross Keys Surgery. Initially he offered me a one-week trial, and funnily enough, he never did officially tell me whether I could stay or not! As it was I was the Practice Nurse for the next twenty-six years! In my time at the Cross Keys I can honestly say that all the doctors, Dr Edwards, Dr Gould, Dr Cooper, Dr Fordham, Dr Hood and then later people like Dr Durban, Dr Maisey and Dr Appleton, were all marvellous to me and I won't hear a word said against any of them. They really were a super team and I enjoyed my time there so much.

In other parts of this book we have referred to a number of characters that have graced the town over the years and Barbara Wharton, the nurse, was indeed a real bubbly character. Everyone loved her and she put even the most nervous patient at their ease when dressing their wounds or giving them an injection. Mind you, being so well-known in the town did have its drawbacks. Barbara recalls:

> I remember once I had to give dear old Frank Sulston an injection in his bottom. 'You can't do that,' he said indignantly, 'I KNOW you!' I had to explain to him that he was no different to anyone else and anyway, he only had to lower his trousers a little bit. He let me do the injection after that!

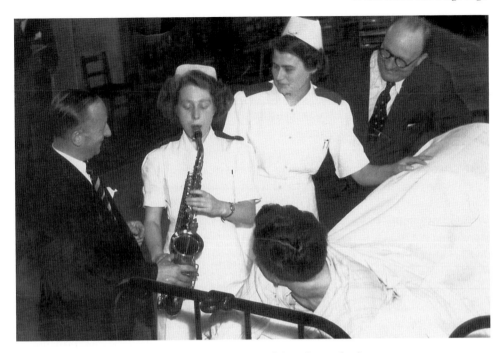

Nurse Barbara plays sax, watched by Billy Cotton (right). Wakey, wakey!

John and Barbara Wharton's wedding day.

Barbara took all her tasks in her stride and became a very good and trusted friend of the town:

> One morning I saw thirty-two patients, ranging from doing blood tests, dressing wounds, ear syringing, injections and all manner of other jobs, including helping the doctors on occasion, sometimes when visiting companies like Ortho's, to help with medicals and the like. It was certainly a job with plenty of variety!

When asked if she could put a finger on how many injections she gave in her career, she replied with a resounding, 'Not a clue!' But one would imagine that it must have run into many thousands.

Her close affinity to Princes Risborough saw her able to deal with many of the well-known faces:

> I remember some of those characters like Charlie Newell, Oscar Wheatley, Frank Purcell, Mrs Fanning, Jim Barefoot and Frank Dean, the policeman. Frank once caught my sister scrumping apples in Chester's field, and said, 'I know it's you, Ann Saunders!' What he didn't realise was that his own daughter, Jean, was also helping Ann! I also worked with some lovely receptionists in the surgery over the years, none more so than Ann Versey. Then there was Connie Titterton, and I remember the vicar stuttering over her name at her wedding, and Valerie Vipond as well, all lovely people. Sadly we had a spate of terrible tragedies amongst those girls all happening around the same time, and it was all very sad. But those girls were all so good to me and I loved them all.

After her twenty-six years at the surgery, Barbara took the opportunity to retire at the same time as her husband John left the railways. 'I felt it would be a good time to end what had been a wonderful career, and I was looking forward to spending some time with John. We had worked so hard over the years and the time was right to share more of our lives together again.'

Sadly that time together was short-lived as John tragically died just four months later. Barbara's redoubtable spirit and determination has seen her overcome some traumatic experiences, and this was yet another. But if you meet her today you will find a lady with an amazing sense of fun and a penchant for laughter that is so infectious. Her bubbly personality is still there and always will be, and her nickname of 'Bubbles', which she picked up as a schoolgirl, is perfectly suited. When remembering John, she said, very tongue-in-cheek, 'You wait til I get up there, I shall give him what for, leaving me so soon!'

John needn't worry. It is more likely he will receive a lovely warm cuddle.

Chapter Ten

A Councillor, Born and Bred

When Eunice Clifford's Mum and Dad, Lucy and Harold Wilkins, decided to move to Princes Risborough from their native Wales during the depression of the 1930s, it was to shape the life of one of the town's most popular councillors. This book often refers to the characters of the town and Eunice definitely falls into that category:

I was actually born in No. 1 Brooke Road just at the start of the war. My Dad had found a job working for Hickman's Transport, which was based at Back Lane, and I vaguely remember living in our house during the war. I can just about recall the street party we had in our road to celebrate the end of the war, and the relief that everyone felt at that time. The house was typical of the period, with a coal shed out the back and a big garden. We were all issued with

The angelic Eunice (née Wilkins) Clifford.

gas masks during those war years and even the kids had one. I remember ours was a Mickey Mouse gas mask, and me and my brother Harold used to wear it if we went into the toilet after Dad! It used to help mask the horrible smells! Life was very hard for everyone then and everything was on ration. I remember once, Dad managed to 'obtain' a box of oranges from one of his loads and he brought it home and hid it under the stairs. He swore us to secrecy, but for some unexplained reason the secret got out and kids from all over the town turned up to try and get one of those oranges.

Hickman's Transport was a good firm to work for; they later became part of British Road Services, and the staff enjoyed lots of out-of-work fun. There was a darts team and a cricket team too. The cricketers used the field just below the chalk pits for their home matches and one of their lorries would drive along the Icknield Way, carrying the tea urn and bringing the sandwiches for tea. When the team played away games, they would all pile into one of the lorries which Hickman's provided. Eunice recalls:

My Dad and my Uncle Johnny used to play for the cricket team and I remember one game when we all piled into the lorry. There was the team, and several of the player's children also went along and one of them, Roz Makepeace, even took her dog, Sue, with us. After the match was finished and the post match entertainment (drinking!) had been completed, we all set off for home. When we arrived back at Risborough we suddenly realised that Sue was not with us! So we had to go all the way back and there was the poor dog, still sat in the car park patiently waiting!

Eunice went to St Mary's Church School and did all the first part of her schooling there:

Hickman's Transport cricket team.

Hickman's lorry.

We used to have to walk up to the Council School, as we called Bell Street, to have our lunch before marching back again for the afternoon lessons. Miss Lees was my first teacher and I also remember Mr Egan and Mr Starkey, who was the Headmaster. Mr Starkey had taken over the role from Emily Hancock. Miss Lees later married Horace Haigh, who was a teacher at Bell Street. The playground at the Church School seemed massive in those days, but when I walk past it today I can't believe how small it all looks. I did enjoy that school though, and we had some great lessons that today's children don't have the chance to enjoy. Where the Mount car park is today used to be just waste ground and there was a tump that we would sit on to do sketching and drawing. We also went on nature walks, as a class and in pairs, holding hands, and we used to love that. My best friends Betty Wixon and Janet Lawrie and I were inseparable in those days until Betty passed for Grammar. Janet and me went on to the Secondary Modern. There are so many fond memories of those school years though, and I particularly enjoyed being the milk monitor, especially on frosty days. Those bottles had two or three inches of 'ice lolly' at the top on some cold mornings! On the way to school we would often be tempted to go into the Manor Farm down the lane by the Church, to see some of the animals. The farmer had a couple of amazing shire horses there as well as his pigs and cows. The shire horses used to graze on what is now Wades Field and I remember one being called Morgan! And there were always some kittens in the farm buildings as well. My Mum used to warn me against going there saying that if I got dirty and smelly before I got to school, she would give me a good hiding!

As for toys, Eunice remembers having a doll's pram, but she was not very girlie and was far happier climbing trees with the boys:

We picked cowslips, bluebells and primroses regularly, and in the winter, when it was frozen, we would skate on the moat, which was over the back of where Tesco's is now. We often found grass snakes and my brother Harold had a pet magpie. That bird was so tame. We called

Manor Farm.

it Maggie and Dad built a run for it, although it was free to fly away at anytime, but it never did and just stayed with us. There was a Mrs Churchill who lived further down the road who didn't like it much though. Every time she walked past our house that bird would go for her and nip the backs of her ankles! She even called the police in, but what could they do, the bird was free to go, it was just her that it didn't like!

As the 1940s moved into the 1950s, Eunice and her friends continued to enjoy their childhood with the freedom that today's children will never understand:

I know when you look back like this, it is easy to just remember the good times, but I can honestly say that we had a wonderful childhood and enjoyed every moment of it. Some days we would be out all day, taking sandwiches up to Whiteleaf Cross, or Pyrtle Springs, with a whole gang of us. We would come home filthy dirty, with our backsides out of our knickers after sliding down the front of the Cross and knickers thick with chalk! But we never worried about being out on our own and we had such fun. I also loved the fêtes that were put on in Back Lane, they were real old-fashioned fêtes and the whole town would turn out to attend. I remember Diana Dors opened one of them and we also had the Dagenham Girl Pipers at another. I also loved Mr Whitney's train rides. He had a big train set with a train that all the people could ride on around the fête site, great fun! And then there was the tug-o-war competition with Albert Young bellowing his instructions to the teams as we all shouted, 'HEAVE!'

We also often used to go up the King George Rec and have a great time. It used to have a pavilion then and the grass was rarely cut but we would be rolling in the long grass and playing simple games and having the time of our lives. But we were all growing up fast by now too, and we were on a voyage of discovery. I remember the Thompson boys, Trevor and Keith, used to join us girls and there was plenty of 'You show me yours and I'll show you mine!' Mind you, after they showed me theirs I ran like hell, and they never did see mine! My Mum used to go mad when I dashed in doors and she found out why. 'I'll sew your knickers to your vest my girl,' she would say to me!

You know how as kids we would build a good trolley, out of old pram wheels? Well, my brother, Harold, and me built a brilliant trolley and we used to go down the Longwick Road to the gasworks with it to see the Thompson boy's Dad, Bob, who used to work there. We used to call him 'Gashouse Bob', that was his nickname. Anyway, we would pick up a bag of coke for our Mum and put it on our trolley and then wheel it back home again. We did love that old trolley.

Kids could be quite cruel at times though and Eunice remembers her and her friends teasing Robin Ball because of his 'posh' voice, and also Dave Purdom for being a Blue Coat schoolboy:

Robin never forgot it, and when he had his shop he often used to remind me about the teasing! He was a lovely bloke though, and I miss him dearly. As for Dave, if truth be told, I fancied him like mad! Every time he came home to Risborough he used to join in the games with our gang and I used to get the other boys to hold him down so I could plant a real smacker of a kiss on him! Another lovely bloke was Dave.

Eunice was one of those who lived through the birth of a life-changing phenomenon that was called rock and roll:

All the kids went mad when they heard all these new songs coming out from their wireless and we loved it. Looking back it was amazing to be in at the beginning and as teenagers we enjoyed Saturday night dances at the Walsingham Hall. Daisy Simmons was the manageress and the Hall was a hotbed of activity. The RAF boys from Wendover would come over and invariably it would end in a fight or two between them and the locals, but despite all that we had a good time most weeks. Molins used to have some great dos in their works' canteen and I remember enjoying those so much too.

The family never ventured far from Princes Risborough, and couldn't afford holidays, just the occasional day trip to the seaside on Townsend Coaches or the like. Eunice does recall once visiting, as a child, the big department store in High Wycombe called Murray's, to see Father Christmas. In the early days it was quite a treat to go to Aylesbury or Wycombe. So it was quite ironic that her first job was in High Wycombe, where she went to work in the office at Broom & Wade. She later returned to Risborough to work at Aston & Full, then Cheverton & Laidler's and then in Bonham's Sweet Shop in the Market Square, which later became the Corner Shop:

I was pretty nervous when I started work, which was unusual for me, but you always had a healthy respect for those who were in charge in those days. In the end though, I much preferred working in a factory environment as opposed to an office. Mind you, when I went to Chev's, I was a bit too clever for my own good. I watched the experienced girls stamping away at their machines, cutting out the packages nine to the dozen, and I thought this looks quite easy. The first go I had, I snapped one of my finger nails clean off!

Like many others in this book, Eunice has fond memories of shopping in the town:

We would go into Adcock & Percival's every Saturday after Dad was paid, to get our groceries. The smells and atmosphere of that shop still lingers in my head to this day, especially the coffee beans roasting. I used to go into Blue Kettle Jack's sweet shop at the bottom of Duke Street a lot too, and again, the smell of their dinner cooking out the back wafted through the shop, and I distinctly remember that. There was Leslie Herman, who had a sign outside announcing him as 'The Shirt King' and I also remember a bookies in Duke Street. Dad used to send me up with his and my Uncle Johnny's bets, warning me not to tell anyone where I was going! It was ironic when my sister-in-law became the first female bookie in the county!

In those days of course, young girls didn't dream of a career, they were more geared to getting married and having children. Eunice was no exception and she married her husband Colin in 1961. 'Three days after my nineteenth birthday,' says Eunice, 'and we've now celebrated forty-eight years of marriage and we have been blessed with three children, Dawn, Nick and Linda. And they said it wouldn't last', added Eunice with guffaws of laughter!

When you spend any time with Eunice you quickly understand that the passion she still feels for Princes Risborough is as keen today as it always has been:

Eunice in her garden with a Townsend coach in the background.

I love the town, and love living here, and I get very angry when I hear people moaning about it. It has changed, of that there is no doubt, but it still has a lot to offer. I feel a little sad that the families are not staying in the town as they used to. At one time several generations of one family would stay and set up home here, but alas these days it is very difficult for the youngsters to afford to live here and the waiting list for housing makes it almost impossible for them to stay. As a result the families, that were once the mainstay of a place like Risborough, are fewer and fewer. The shops too have changed and Risborough, once a bustling, busy shopping centre, is now struggling, not only to attract new business but also to attract the right sort of businesses. Whether it will change again, remains to be seen. I personally hope it does, but I have my doubts. Times are so different now, in my day when our Mum and Dad said they were broke, they were broke, and had no money at all. But also in those days, everyone helped out, and if a person was in trouble then you could rely so much on your neighbours.

One story sums up what I'm trying to say. I remember my Dad had been off work ill and no money was coming in, there was no sick pay in those days. We actually went a couple of weeks without going into Adcock & Percival's for groceries, as Mum had no money. One night there was a knock at the door and Mr Percival was stood there, asking Mum why we hadn't been in for groceries for a couple of weeks. Mum explained the situation and Mr Percival said that we should come up to the shop and order some groceries and he would sort something out for us. Now, how kind was that? Can you imagine Mr Tesco doing that? It just shows you how different the community spirit was then and how genuine the Princes Risborough traders could be.

All of this passion for the town was channelled into the right direction in October 2001 when, having had the seeds of joining the council team sewn in her mind by John Coombes, Dave Allworth then asked Eunice to stand for election when a vacancy arose. She duly did and was co-opted on. Later, there was an election and she polled third place with an excellent number of votes proving her popularity, and she has served the town diligently ever since.

Spend an hour in Eunice's company and we guarantee you will end up laughing! Her storytelling is unique, and to be honest, the tales she can recount could fill quite a few of these books. You cannot possibly question the love and affection she has for the town of Princes Risborough, and we say long may that continue.

Chapter Eleven

The Literary Institute – A Mystery to Many

One of the most mysterious, and yet most important, buildings in Princes Risborough is situated halfway down the High Street opposite the iconic Wainwright's shoe shop. Over the years, few people would have seen anyone go in there, and even fewer knew what lay behind those black front doors. We are talking about the Literary Institute, a building that was, on 27 February 1891, presented to the people of the town in a glittering opening ceremony.

The Literary Institute.

It had been built by Lord Rothschild, at a cost of £1,200, and the formal opening was held in a large room on the ground floor. Unfortunately Lord Rothschild was in London on business and could not be present, so his wife, Lady Rothschild, did the honours. The Reverend H. W. Meeres, from St Mary's Church, invited her to announce the opening and during a pleasant speech she said:

> I have the greatest pleasure in declaring the Institute open and I wish that every success might attend its future. I am sorry that Lord Rothschild has been detained by his business in London, and I am sure that he would rather be here, as it would be a double pleasure being amongst his old friends. He has many pleasant memories of Princes Risborough and so many people here had been kind enough to give their votes to Nathaniel Rothschild. It has been a real pleasure for him to provide this Institute and I hope it will be a constant source of pleasure and profit to all who resorted to it.

She went on to say how pleased she was that the institute would be open to ladies and gentlemen as she did not approve of any building that was only open to gentlemen! That remark brought applause from the audience.

There was to be hope that a circulating library may one day be on the premises and Lady Rothschild even offered to send some books to start the library off. It was agreed by all at the gathering that full use would be made of the building, for learning and for entertainment. With that the whole party adjourned upstairs to 'partake in a most enjoyable luncheon provided by Messrs J.C. Garner & Co., the well-known caterers from Aylesbury.'

After the meal further speeches were made with the Reverend Meeres proposed as 'Chairman' and in his reply, the vicar said:

> I have to get through a good deal of public speaking, on all sorts of subjects, but there is one subject I cannot speak upon, and that is about myself. I find that the subject is neither interesting, picturesque, nor inspiring. [*Laughter*] It is a subject I can never handle. If I try to be pathetic, people laugh, if I try to be humorous, they weep and if I try to be solemn and impressive, they yawn and take out their watches! [*Laughter*] Therefore I can only say that I thank them for the compliment and I will always do my best for Princes Risborough.

So, the new Literary Institute was born and from that day to this, the building has been used for a number of different functions. Lord Rothschild leased it to the town at a peppercorn rent for 1,000 years. The interior retains many of the original features, such as the wood panelling around the walls and the unique ornamental fireplaces. In fact, some would say that the building is stuck in a time warp. But it also has an air of tranquillity that is perfectly suited to the snooker room and the reading room, and the building in general.

Over the years lots of events have been held there, including rummage sales, dance groups and ladies' keep-fit classes. Twice a week you could pay your electric bills in the back room, and on other occasions the local tradesmen could have their scales calibrated there. It was not unusual, in years gone by, to see one of the Risborough shopkeepers lugging their heavy scales down to the Literary Institute to have them checked and calibrated.

Upstairs, the former courtroom.

But one of the most important duties that the building performed was as the the local Magistrate's Court. Both before and after the Second World War, the proceedings were held upstairs, and when you go in there today you can envisage how it would have looked. The raised stage at one end was where the magistrates sat, and one can imagine the solemnity of the cases. They certainly dealt with a variety of offences and Eunice Clifford remembers a couple involving her family:

> I remember once, my Mum called my Dad and said that she could see the wireless licence chap outside. Dad knew he didn't have a licence for his wireless at the time and without hesitation he dashed round to the Post Office to get one, as fast as his legs could carry him! Unfortunately, when he returned, the licence man duly arrived and said that it was too late and that he would have to report him anyway. Dad was later duly summoned and he had to attend the Magistrates Court at the Institute. Mr Vaughan was on the bench that day, and he fined my Dad 5s for not having a licence! On another occasion my husband, Colin, and his friend, John Lacey, were also both fined in the same courtroom. Their offence? They were walking home from Risborough to Lacey Green, where we lived, after a 'happy' night at the pub, and when they walked past the Police Station along the Wycombe Road, the police came out and charged them with 'singing in the street and disturbing the peace!' Well, I suppose it was a bit late!

The Magistrate's Court remained there for a number of years with some important townspeople sitting on the bench. Names like Captain Stratton and Mr Stratford-Reed, amongst others, officiated, and it was quite a daunting experience if you appeared before

The snooker room.

them. The court remained until the mid-1960s, when it was decided that the upstairs floor could not support the weight of all the people who attended the day's proceedings, and so it moved out of Risborough. The floor has now been reinforced, but that room is rarely used these days. Many of us in the town who would love to see a Princes Risborough Museum see it as a possible and perfect venue for a display. Meanwhile, the members will continue to enjoy the facilities, play some snooker, have a quiet read, or sit in the spacious and well-kept garden.

Unfortunately, as with many organisations these days, the institute is struggling to attract new members. Not only that, but it's also struggling to find members who would be willing to take on some of the organising roles. As one of the trustees, Dennis Eggleton points out:

> The people running it now are, sadly, all getting older, and we need some new young blood to get involved and help keep the facility open. The institute is open to everyone in Risborough and we, in turn, are open to all new suggestions for its usage. But we would also need help to organise those suggestions.

It would be a crying shame if the facility was lost to the town as the Literary Institute has, indeed, been an institution.

Chapter Twelve

Adcock & Percival - Another Risborough Institution

All through this book, whenever shopping in Princes Risborough is mentioned, then invariably the name of Adcock & Percival's General Store comes up. Every single one of the people we have interviewed has voiced so many fond memories of shopping there. They were particularly keen to remember the smells, the floorboards, the upstairs, the atmosphere and the staff at the shop, so we felt it was worth a short chapter all of its own.

The origins of the family store are unclear, but Samuel Adcock ran it for many years before the war and then Harold Percival's father took over the shop before Harold himself became the owner. He carried it through the post-war years and made it into the shop it became. Harold was formerly a tea taster in London before joining the local business in Risborough. He was to keep the name of Adcock in the business title and funnily enough, the shop was always to be known as Adcocks.

One of the people who worked there for many years was Ada Beckett, or Ada Poulton as she was then. She still lives in Risborough and recalls:

I started work there, the day after Boxing Day 1944, having left school that Christmas at the age of fourteen. I lived in Askett at the time and I worked there until 1958, when I got married. Even after marrying my husband George, I returned part-time and did many more years with Mr Percival. I was taken on as a shop assistant in the grocery section, although for the first three months I wasn't allowed to serve a customer, oh no, in those days you had to be properly trained before you could serve the customers. Rationing was still in force when I started. There were green ration books for children, blue for older children and a buff-coloured one for adults. Every Saturday afternoon, Audrey Clark and me would go into the back office, counting the points and sweet coupons, and also the emergency coupons. Emergency coupons were given to people who wanted their rations in a different shop to the one where they were registered to use them. Whenever the customers used their rations, their books would be stamped so that they were unable to use them twice.

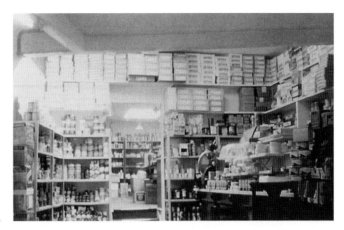

Inside Adcock's grocery store.

During our conversation with Ada, she often used the phrase 'over the other side'. This was a reference to the other departments in the shop, which to her, working in the grocery department, was 'over the other side'. There you would find newspapers, sweets, toys and fancy goods, whilst upstairs Adcock's sold prams and also had a model railway layout on display. Mind you, when Ada first started at Adcock's, the upstairs was a billiard room. The wooden flooring was also fondly remembered by all who went into the shop, as it creaked loudly when you walked around the store.

Ada continues:

The grocery store sold everything; provisions, potatoes, tinned goods, paraffin and coffee. At Christmas we always had some lovely things on sale and I especially remember the Christmas crackers we sold, they were always a bit special. The coffee beans in the roasting machine emanated a familiar smell to every resident, but the machine also caused a problem or two at times. I remember on several occasions we almost had to send for the Fire Brigade as flames appeared! Luckily we always managed to sort it out, which was just as well because, ironically, Mr Percival was actually in the Fire Brigade and manned the station when the engine went out from its base, then in Church Street. There was another occasion when Mr Percival detected a burning smell, but it had nothing to do with the coffee machine. Audrey and me had been craftily roasting chestnuts and crumpets on the electric fire and Mr Percival came in and asked if we could smell burning. We didn't dare tell him what we had been doing!

Do you know, we used to send those coffee beans all over the country. We had customers in Scotland, Cornwall and all sorts of other places and we would bag up the order and take them round to the Post Office to be shipped off. If that was one of the first businesses to start mail order, then Adcock's also had a delivery service locally that would be the envy of any Tesco store these days! We used to deliver to many of the other famous traders of the town, like the Goodearls, the Easts and Frank Gray. All week we used to make up orders and deliver all round Risborough, and we used to send to all the outlying villages too, like Longwick, Loosley Row, Lacey Green and Butlers Cross. People used to phone in their orders or bring their order books into the shops. Also, three mornings a week, Audrey Clark and me used to go out on our bikes on our rounds, to visit some of our customers and pick up their orders

Adcock's staff on a float for the Queen's Coronation parade.

from their houses. We would then go back to the shop and make up the orders ready for Dan Ashford to deliver in the shop van. Originally the van was actually an ordinary car which had a box fitted to the back. If Dan was ever on holiday, we would hire Audrey's brother, Will, who worked for Benyon's Garage, to do the driving. Later on though, we had a proper van, and after I had learned to drive, I used to help deliver the goods myself. In fact it was Dan Ashford who taught me to drive, and I even took my driving test in that shop van!

Typically, in years gone by, all the shopkeepers helped each other out. Ada recalls:

Occasionally, when we were making up the grocery orders, we would find we had run out of corn flakes or something. We did no more than go up to Bloss's shop and they would give us enough packets to satisfy our orders. Then, when we received our next order, we would take the same amount of boxes back to Bloss's. This happened a lot between the various shops, everyone helped each other. One thing that always worries me in modern shops is what they do when there is a power cut? Everything is so electrically mechanised now compared to the manual tills we had. These days the big supermarkets close when there is a power cut. But in our day, out would come the candles and it would be business as usual!

As a shopkeeper, Harold Percival was certainly heavily involved in the local community, as, amongst other things, he was also a Scout Master and Secretary of the Lawn Tennis Club in Back Lane. He was always involved when special events came along too. He organised a terrific float for the Queen's 1953 Coronation parade through the town, on a horse and cart borrowed from Lacey's the builders in Duke Street. The end came for the shop when Harold retired around 1978 and sold the premises, which was later turned into three smaller units.

Hickman's float
for the Coronation
parade.

Adcock & Percival's
staff.

The much missed
Adcock & Percival's
store.

The staff at the shop were all well-liked, and all retained their own happy memories of their own time working there. You may well remember some of the names of those former Adcock's staff members: Sheila Clay, Dan Ashford, Min Phipps, Betty Bonner, Jessie Burrows, Stan Collier, John Redrup, John Little, Cliff Dancer, Audrey Clark, Mrs Carter, Godfrey Packwood, Gladys Hajdukovicz, Mrs Williams, Ann Phipps and Angela Phipps. And, of course, there was Ada, who we thank for one last memory:

> I felt that Harold Percival was not only my boss, but also a good friend, and I often babysat for his two children, Graham and Judy. I was really sad when he died a few years back, but he is still in the community as he is buried in Monks Risborough churchyard.

The closure of Adcock & Percival's was the end of an era, but not the end of all the memories, and rarely has a shop in Princes Risborough enjoyed such a long-lasting affection from the people of the town. There are many other fond memories of the shop featured throughout this book and it will probably never be forgotten.

Ada Beckett, former Adcock & Percival's shop assistant, marries George Poulton at St Mary's Church in October 1958.

Chapter Thirteen

The Last Days of Steam

Ever since the railways first came to Princes Risborough in 1862, the line has been developed into a vital connection to the capital and the rest of the country, and a source of great economic wealth for the town. Those of you who see our station today could never imagine how busy and important the site has been over the years, especially during the steam days immediately after the war, through to the 1960s.

One man who remembers that period and played a part in the running of the station is Dave Pinfold. Dave originally came from Fritwell, in North Oxfordshire, and first joined the Great Western Railway in 1947 at the age of seventeen, working at Ardley, 'When I first started at Ardley as a trainee, I was on just £5 2s 0d per week. I wanted to be a signaller, but you had to be eighteen before you could take on that role. However, they were so desperate for new signallers they took me on at seventeen-and-a-half.'

Naturally, signalling was not something you could go into without proper training, and Dave had to go to the Signal School at Reading to learn his craft, and after that, a four-month-long intensive course to learn all the rules and regulations. Dave did the course and passed successfully but unfortunately, these were also the days of National Service, and in 1948 Dave had to do his stint:

I was luckier than some because I only did just under eighteen months in the Army, serving with the King's Shropshire Light Infantry. They sent us to Hong Kong once, but almost as quickly as we had arrived, we were on our way home again! After we got back to Southampton we were told we were being demobbed, but my regiment actually went out to Korea shortly afterwards, so I was not sorry to miss that.

When Dave finished his Army service he returned to the railways, and Ardley signal box for a short time, but then around 1950 he saw the opportunity of a job advertised at Princes Risborough and he decided to try his luck.

Dave recalls:

When I saw that advert I thought it was worth a try. Everyone told me not to apply, but I did, and to my surprise managed to get the job. All signallers' pay was graded and we all started on Grade Five, but the Risborough South Box was a Grade Three, quite a bit more money, so coming to Risborough certainly changed my life, in more ways than one. There were two signal boxes at Risborough, the South Box and the North Box. They were both on different pay grades and you earned more working in the larger North Box, but I started in the other one. It has gone now, but was situated before the Horsenden Bridge and at the end of engine sheds and shunting track at the bottom end of where the car park is now. I shared a shift with another chap and I really started to learn about signalling in that box. We had a lot of traffic in the station in those days, from express trains going through to the north, to local traffic going to Chinnor, Watlington, Thame and Aylesbury, and even a small branch line to the Forest Laboratory. From the South Box we handled all the shunting and local stuff switching the points and sorting out what was going where. The line to Watlington was quite busy and it served the Chinnor Cement Works, so there were a lot of freight wagons, mostly coal, going that way. We had three shifts and I loved it in those early days. You were always so busy in the early 1950s. A lot of the freight came out of Woodford or Banbury through here. We were always doing a lot of short section work and we were lucky at Risborough because we had a mass of complicated track within a short space around the station, so it was all good practice for newcomers like myself.

When Dave first came to Risborough he stayed at lodgings, but then in the later part of the 1950s his life was to change again when he met his wife. Elizabeth Langston, or Betty as she is known, was born and bred in Monks Risborough. Betty remembers:

I was born in a house opposite the Post office along the Aylesbury Road and went to school at Monks Risborough, in fact I actually took Dennis Eggleton [another of the people featured in this book] to school on his first day. My Mum and my sister went there, and my daughter too, and I even did a stint as a dinner lady, so we have always had a close affinity with that school.

Betty's Uncle was a manager at Dorsett's grocery store in Princes Risborough and another Uncle managed Jefferies the butchers, in Duke Street, and she also remembers the dances held at the Walsingham Hall with great affection. Betty's family was a local one as her father came from Longdown Farm at Kimble. She says:

As kids we used to go to the park, now called the King George V Park, to play. I remember the Princes Risborough kids telling us that as we were from Monks Risborough, we weren't allowed to play there. We ignored them and kept coming back to play anyway. I do have many happy memories of living in Risborough and another that sticks in my mind is seeing old Will Tappin delivering coal with his horse and cart. He used to get off the cart and the horse knew exactly where to go and would walk the round without any help from Will. It was amazing.

Dave and Betty eventually met at the Carlton Cinema in Risborough, one of the many romances that blossomed after meeting at that cinema, no doubt. After they married, in

1957, they lived for a time in the Prefabs at the bottom of Brooke Road. They have lived at their current address, also in Brooke Road, for the last forty-five years, and they have now been married for fifty-two years.

One of the things that attracted Dave to the railways was his love of the many different engines and rolling stock. During our interview he often waxed lyrical about the types of trains that came through the station. In recent years we have had the occasional much-heralded visit from the *Royal Scot* or the *Sir Nigel Gresley* through from London, but in those days Dave often had the *Royal Scot* through. The trains would come out of Paddington and go on to Wolverhampton or Sheffield, eventually on their way to Scotland. Dave stayed for two years in the South Box, but then a chance arose to transfer to the North Box and he was to stay there for the rest of his working life. Dave remembers:

Again we had three shifts and I used to relieve John Wharton, although I knew him as Sid Wharton. We always called him Sid! On the Day Turn or Late Turn we also had a booking lad and his job would be to keep the train register and use it to remind the signalman of the position of trains within the section at any time. Most of the lads we had with us went on to become signallers themselves. We had some smashing lads working there and one of my best mates was a former POW who came from Romania called Michael Kumas. He was a great bloke who was able to turn his hand to all sorts of things. He was a godsend to us at Risborough and was brilliant at improvising, very useful when things broke down. We were always so busy in that North Box and had little time to sit down. We had 126 levers in there, and the frame they sat in was exactly the same length as a cricket pitch, 22 yards. On the down line you had express trains to Birkenhead, Wolverhampton and Shrewsbury on the hour and on top of that you had all the local trains. A couple of trains would turn off at Ashendon, the 12.15 and the 6.15 Marylebone to Sheffield expresses. You had to be careful, because the 6.15 from Marylebone and the 6.10 from Paddington used to arrive at Risborough almost together and you had to make sure you routed each of them in their right direction.

The North Box had a toilet, sink and a small Belling cooker. There were some wooden seats too, but the lads in the box soon brought in a few home comforts, like armchairs. Dave says:

I remember when I first went there the remains of an air-raid shelter was still on the side of the box, where they later put the toilet. And there was an old desk in the box and every year the house martins would turn up to nest on the signal box and the first day they arrived each year I wrote it down on that desk. If the desk is still in there, then you could see my writing. We sometimes had thirteen or fourteen nests on that box, but do you know, after we left and it was finally shut down, those martins never returned to nest there. We did have some fun in that box over the years though, especially when we had a good booking lad with us. We used to toss a coin to see who would walk down the other end of the lever frame to pull the lever to signal the down train. And we used to have these lever collars that we would roll to each other up and down the highly polished floor.

There were one or two unofficial things that went on in that signal box too. In our research with various people for this book we talked to Harold Mitchell, and as soon as we mentioned

The North Signal Box.

the large signal box at Risborough station he said, 'I used to have my hair cut there!' This puzzled us, until we found out that Dave Pinfold occasionally cut people's hair. He says, 'I used to go into Wally Burton's shop for my own hair to be cut, but after he finished mine I used to cut his for him. I must admit I did do an occasional haircut at work too.'

Another of the jobs for the booking lad was as token runner. The tokens had to be handed to the engine drivers as they passed. The tokens were an aid to being able to identify exactly where each train was at any given time, very important to the signaller of course. Only the trains that went along the branch lines were given these, and not the express through-trains.

Dave particularly remembers the difficulties of the harsh winter of 1963:

That was the toughest time that I ever had in my job as a signaller. It was horrendous and there was chaos everywhere. We couldn't shift the points because everything was so frozen up and as soon as we cleared the snow a new lot would fall and cover them all again. It was a nightmare! We used to have a milk train come through during the night from Dorrington, en route for Marylebone. But on one of these snowy nights the train got stuck between Risborough and Ashendon. In the end they sent one of the new diesel trains to try and pull it free and that got stuck too. They had to call the Army in from Arncott to dig the trains out.

Betty remembered that winter too as it was around that time that Berndene School opened in Wellington Avenue, 'My daughter was due to start there and none of the paths were clear, it was horrendous.'

Dave on the phone to the 'Fat Controller'.

We ask if Dave had any unusual experiences as a signaller. He replies:

I used to walk backwards and forwards to work along the railway line, they would probably shoot you for doing that today! But nearly every night, when I came home, this fox would follow me all the way along the line. I was also the bloke in the signal box on the day that Witcher's Garage caught fire and I was the one who called the Fire Brigade. I'm not sure how the fire started, I think it was something to do with a welder, but boy, did that garage go up in flames and I had a ringside seat! And do you remember the Railway Arms? It was a pub that was half on railway property and half on private property. It was a unique wooden building half-owned by the railway. Anyway, after it was closed down and boarded up, the new diesel trains came into service. Suddenly the old pub was deemed a fire hazard. The fact that the old steam trains, which threw out all the fire and brimstone from their steam boilers and fireboxes, had gone past trouble free for years, it was now decided that the pub was a fire risk! So it was then demolished. Very strange.

Another time Dave recalls a near disaster at the station:

This lorry driver was passing and noticed that a hole had suddenly appeared under the track, right next to the South Box. He phoned the station and they quickly phoned me in the North Box. I nearly died, as I knew the 8.55 Birkenhead express was due through Risborough at any moment. I dashed along the lever frame and pulled every single lever over. Luckily the driver

Dave Pinfold and John Wharton on their last day in the signal box before it was shut down.

of the express saw the signals and managed to stop the train just a couple of coach lengths short of the hole. That averted what might have been a really nasty accident. The engine was 6008 *King James II*, if my memory serves me right.

There were a few other incidents at the station, which were dealt with locally, including a shunting mistake that led to a whole row of freight wagons being derailed. Overall though, the highly professional expertise of all the lads in the signal boxes saw to it that a smooth and efficient service was provided for the many passengers who used the trains at Princes Risborough station.

It was a sad day for Dave when the North Box was closed down and it signalled [pardon the pun!] the end of his working life:

My health had been deteriorating for a while, and when they decided to close the signal box down and move all signalling operations back to Marylebone, I called it a day. They desperately wanted all of us signallers to go to London and work there, but I knew I was not physically up to it at the time so I took redundancy. I had completed forty-five years service on the railways and I had experienced so many changes through that time, surviving Dr Beeching's axe, and seeing the death of steam, amongst many other things. When the box signalled its last train through I realised it was the end. I loved the job when I started, but over the years, management changes, coupled with all the new rules and regulations, made it all less enjoyable. Those glorious days of steam will never be seen again, and I for one mourn their passing. Thankfully though, Risborough station survives and is still a valuable asset to the town.

Dave and Betty are now great-grandparents, and Dave has enough hobbies to keep 100 people busy. He says finally:

Do you know, I've always had lots of hobbies, and collected things that I love, and I also had a huge garden that I maintained, as well as a large allotment on the Longwick Road, and I produced all my own vegetables. How on earth did I find the time to go to work? I don't know.

Chapter Fourteen

A Sporting Chance

One feature of Princes Risborough life that has always been prominent is the sporting scene. There have been many football and cricket teams, and many other sports have been catered for in the schools and the youth clubs around the area. Some fine sportsmen and women have represented the town, and occasionally there has been exceptional talent on view. One of the longest and most inspiring sporting careers belongs to the evergreen Colyn Makepeace, perennially and affectionately known to all as 'Nibbo.' We asked him how he gained his long-lasting nickname and it transpired that 'Nibbo' was a term for a little tearaway [or 'little sod' as Nibbo himself put it!]. 'That was me, apparently,' said Nibbo, 'so it stuck. Mind you, a few years ago, when I was training the Risborough Rangers Under-10s team, a new Mum came up to me with a little lad and said she was told to ask for "Yobbo"!'

Nibbo was born in Kingsmead in Monks Risborough after his Mum, Doris, and Dad, Walter, settled there. They had originally come from Haddenham and Nether Winchendon before coming to Risborough, and there are still many family members in that area. After coming to live in Monks, the Makepeace clan went on to have a huge influence in and around Princes Risborough, with Doris, who first joined the Red Cross, becoming a nurse at Stoke Mandeville for over twenty years. Nibbo's Dad worked for Hickman's transport in Risborough, before eventually joining Crockett's Transport, where he worked for many years driving a tanker delivering the milk from farms to the milk depots. He was a keen sportsman and was involved with the local sporting teams for as long as Nibbo can remember, at one time being Chairman of Monks Risborough Football Club. His Dad was actually one of nineteen children and, as a result, there are Makepeace relations all round the area.

Nibbo's Mum also started the Red Cross in Risborough and was always involved in any number of organisations and groups. She later helped form the Darby and Joan club in Risborough, many years ago. Nibbo recalls:

They used to go on these coach holidays to the seaside or somewhere like that, and Mum would go along to help supervise all the elderly folk. It was quite sad really, because there was more than one occasion when she counted them all on the bus okay, but on the way back there would be an empty seat because one of the folk had died during the week!

From a very early age, the young Nibbo was sport mad. He recalls:

It was football in the winter and cricket in the summer. We would play in the street for any number of hours. We didn't have to worry much about cars coming down the road, they were so few and far between, and we rarely had to move the goalposts or stumps. In fact, we knew almost to the minute when certain cars would turn up! And if you lived in Monks Risborough you usually played for Monks at both sports. I remember going to watch Monks play football, and sometimes they were one short so I would get a game, and that is how I started playing proper football. It was the same at cricket too. Mum used to do the cricket teas with Mrs Carter and I would go to watch the game. Again, I might be roped in to play if they were short, although it didn't take much persuasion. I also remember vividly going to watch Dad play for Hickman's Works' cricket team, in a field off the Icknield Way. But my earliest memories of playing football was when I played for Kingsmead in the Princes Risborough Tenants Association Cup. It was played for between street teams from Monks and Princes Risborough and I remember we won that cup once with lads from our street like Freddie Ridgeway, Alfie Redding, some of the Carter boys and John Williams, who lived up on the Aylesbury Road. The Carter boy's Mum, Mrs Jessie Carter, was the manager, and it was

The Princes Risborough Red Cross with Mrs Makepeace (left).

The Darby and Joan members.

so exciting because we actually took the cup home on the train, between Risborough station and Monks Risborough halt!

When playing cricket, players often have curious superstitious rituals they have when they are batting, but Nibbo will always be remembered by all those that played with him for the most eccentric of habits. Just before the bowler bowled the ball, Nibbo would tap the end of his bat on his boot twice, raise the bat to the heavens and point it at a bit of blue sky, then touch his nose with his hand and then settle for the delivery. Now that was okay with a fast bowler, but when it was a slow bowler Nibbo had to hurry it up a bit. His team-mates were used to it, but some of the bowlers would stop dead in their tracks thinking he wasn't ready. Often he wasn't, as his shattered stumps would testify!

Nibbo has fond memories of the railway:

We often used to travel into Aylesbury on the train and in those old steam days, I was able to travel with the driver in the engine. They let you in those days, no health and safety worries then! Mum used to go mad at me because I was black by the time we reached home. Out would come her hanky, a bit of spit and a quick wipe round of the face, hands and knees! Do you know, to this day, I hate washing my knees! I also remember if sometimes me and my mates missed the last train home, we would then walk back to Monks Risborough on the railway line. The sleepers were just too far apart to make it in one step and it was quite tricky in the dark walking along the line. And of course you had to keep looking over your shoulder and listening carefully in case a train came down the

The Kingsmead boys team with the manageress, Mrs Carter.

line. Looking back it was so dangerous, but at the time we never thought anything of it really. Today we would probably be put in prison for doing it, but in those days it was the quickest route home.

Growing up in Kingsmead was great fun for Nibbo, as he and his mates were so close. It was one huge family in that street as everyone knew each other and helped each other out in times of trouble. They all went to Monks Risborough School and they all remember their time there with great affection. Nibbo stayed at the school until he was eleven and then went on to finish the rest of his schooling at Bell Street, for two years, and then, at the newly opened Top School. He left school at fifteen and by then the town was his 'patch'. He has many fond memories of tramping across the fields, which is now the Place Farm estate, to visit Blue Kettle Jack's sweet shop, or going to the Carlton Cinema for his seat in the one and threes!

We walked everywhere in those days of course, although we did use the bus on occasions. I got told off by the bus conductor, Mr Hearn, one day, because I sat down on the bus and asked him for one return ticket please. 'Where to?' he asked. 'Back here of course.' I answered. He clipped me round the ear for being so cheeky. I also always invariably had my hair cut by Wally Burton, and do you know, even to this day we still say in our house, pull the Wally's when we want the curtains pulled. Wally Burton's – curtains, get it? And whilst going back home to Mum we would be told to pop in to Eggleton's Bakery to buy a loaf. It was almost impossible to carry one of their loaves home without pinching a bit to eat!

MRCC tea ladies.

Playing sport in those days was a lot more difficult than it is today, especially with away fixtures. Nibbo recalls:

> Nobody had cars then and when we played for Monks Risborough football team we would often travel to away games in one of Farmer's Coaches, who were based along the Aylesbury Road. We used to hire one of their coaches for away matches. Most of our games were in the Aylesbury District League, along the flat vale, but when we had to go towards Wycombe for a cup game, then it caused a few more problems. As we hit the Pitches going out of Risborough, old Farmer used to tell us all to rock backwards and forwards to help the bus make it to the top of the hill. And on some occasions we even had to get out and push!

Much as he would have liked to, Nibbo could not turn his sporting skills into a career, and after leaving school he had to find a job. One day, when his Mum was at a WI meeting, she was chatting to another lady, who was the wife of local plumber, Arnold Bradbury. She happened to mention that Nibbo wanted to join the building trade and Mr Bradbury was looking for new people. The following Monday, Nibbo joined his friends, Bob Carter and Clive Lipyeart, who were already working for Arnold Bradbury. 'It was the start of my apprenticeship and a life in plumbing,' says Nibbo, 'I did five years as an apprentice and then set up a business with Bob, forming Carter & Makepeace. For the next ten years we built the business up and worked hard, but also found time to enjoy our football and cricket.'

As the 1950s moved into the 1960s, more football teams appeared in the town, with Risborough Rovers taking over from the now defunct Parkfield Rovers, and Risborough

Nibbo (front left) in the cross-country running team.

Monks Risborough or 'Carter' FC.

Tenants being formed from the old Tenants Association. Risborough Football Club became Risborough Town and had their new headquarters and ground at the Windsor Playing Fields in Horsenden. Nibbo recalls:

> It was a chap named Professor Keaton, a member of one of those government think tanks, who was responsible for the town having Windsor Playing Fields. At one time there was a big slope on the whole piece of land, but he arranged for the football pitch to be levelled and we ended up with a good cricket pitch, a football pitch and room too for tennis courts. All are

still used extensively today, all thanks to Professor Keaton. He was also a director at a Football League club and was a founder member of the new Hellenic League, formed in 1953, which Risborough Town FC eventually joined.

There were many excellent footballers and cricketers playing in Risborough during those years and quite a few characters too. Nibbo remembers:

> Some of those lads took their sport very seriously and were very intense, whilst others were so laid back about it they nearly fell over! Two extremes were Mick Orchard and Chris Wilkins. I remember once when we were playing cricket for Monks against Princes Risborough we saw an example of Mick Orchard's thinking. Jack Carter, a brilliant cricketer, was batting and almost winning the game single-handed. It looked odds on a victory for us, but on the last ball of the penultimate over, Jack hit the ball to Mick for a single to take the strike for the last over. But Mick had already thought it through and promptly threw the ball to the boundary, giving Jack a four, but taking him off strike for that last over. That was how Mick used to play his cricket. As for Chris Wilkins, well, Wilkie was something different again. Always the practical joker and instigator of most of the nicknames at the club, on one occasion I actually got one over Wilkie. I remember I had to pick him up for an Easter Monday football match, which was kicking off in the morning. I went round his house at about nine o'clock only to find Wilkie still in bed. His Dad was by the back door cleaning his boots, whilst his Mum cooked his breakfast. Spoilt rotten he was! Anyway, his Mum shouted upstairs to tell him that his breakfast was ready. By the time he came down, I had eaten it!

Footballers in Princes Risborough had plenty of choice in the decades from 1950 to 1980 and invariably played for most clubs in turn. Nibbo was no exception and he played for Monks Risborough and Risborough Town for several years. Later though, he continued to play at a high level after he joined Waddesdon, who were also then in the Hellenic League, and then he had a spell with Hazells, the works' team from Aylesbury:

> I did play in an excellent standard of football for most of my playing career, although I was troubled by dodgy knees in the latter part. I also played with and against some brilliant players, but I knew my level of skill after I once had a trial with Wycombe Wanderers. I then realised that the step up in class was a little too much for me, which is why I remained a plumber!

At twenty-three, Nibbo was asked to take on a player-manager's role with Risborough Town, and this was to give him good experience in running a team, something he developed again later in his life when he managed the Molins team. His two boys, Chris and Daniel, needless to say, were also keen footballers, with Chris once having a spell in Chelsea's youth team. Ferrying his boys from game to game took up much of his time when they were younger, but it gave Nibbo the chance to meet lots of new people in football and strike up long-lasting friendships. Even now he is at retirement age, Nibbo still plays in the occasional veteran's or charity match, and he is heavily involved in bringing on the next generation of footballers with his coaching of Risborough's youngsters. It helps keep him in touch with the game he has loved all his life and keeps him fit too.

Nibbo remembers England's World Cup win in 1966 with a mixture of joy and sadness:

I bought tickets for all eleven games in England's group, they cost me a lot of money at the time, £7 10s 0d! I went to all the England games, including the final as well. It was a magic time, but also it was a sad time for me because my Dad was suffering with cancer and was quite ill. But the family did not want Dad to suspect how ill he was and insisted that I went to the football matches. Dad would have wanted that too and England's ultimate triumph was something I will never ever forget. A few years later, I went to a theatre to see some of the players make a personal appearance. Several players were there and also Kenneth Wolstenholme, the BBC commentator, was also appearing. It is one of my claims to fame that, in a question and answer part of the show, I asked him if he would say those famous words for me. He asked my name and said, 'Nibbo, they think it's all over, it is now!' He actually said it to me! Dad would have loved that!

Behind every great sportsman they say, there is a sporting widow, and in Nibbo's case it is his wife Marion, a Risborough character in her own right, as you will see later in this book. They met at Kimble Youth Club in the Stewart Hall and the romance began when Nibbo took her home on his scooter. However, that initial romance did end, but then about ten years later they got together again and this time they married. Marion's family had arrived in the town when Molins factory was set up in the early 1950s. She recalls:

We were the first family to arrive from Deptford, in London, to settle here and it was difficult for us. I was about eight at the time and coming from the city to the country was a daunting prospect. It took a while for us to settle into country life and to be accepted by the folk of Risborough, but in the end we achieved it and by meeting and marrying Nibbo, I suppose I now qualify as a local!

The area in and around Princes Risborough has always been blessed with many sports-mad people like Nibbo, all playing their part in keeping sport going in the area. People like Derek Wallace, Bob Raynor, Richard Woodward, Ken Shepherd, Harold Mitchell, Roger Ridgeway, John Williams, Ian Austin, Ray Agace, Geoff Mitchell, Colin Steptoe, Pete Boland, Brian Peel, Roy Stratford, Roger Smith and Douglas Miller. Even co-author Mike Payne must receive a mention here, along with a host of other never to be forgotten names. They have all contributed to sport in the town and their dedication should not be underestimated. They have helped give so much entertainment and enjoyment to the sportsmen and women of Princes Risborough. We salute them all.

Chapter Fifteen

It's Been a Busy Life

Co-author Mike Payne has known Harold Mitchell almost from the first day he moved to Princes Risborough from his native Isle of Wight, in the autumn of 1963. He recalls:

> There was a knock on our front door one evening, which my Mum answered. When she opened the door Harold was stood there and said that he had heard that there was a lad who lived here who wanted to play football. That was me, fourteen years old and as keen as mustard. And that was how I started my Princes Risborough football career. Harold was tapping me up to play for his team, Risborough Tenants, a team he had helped form in 1960. From that moment on, that familiar Wolverhampton accent was to play a large part in my life.

Contrary to some people's belief, Harold did not come from Wolverhampton, but was in fact born in Bledlow village in 1917. Harold remembers:

> I was born in a house at the crossroads that went from Risborough to Chinnor one way, up to the Lions pub another and down to Skittle Green the other. Soon after I was born we actually moved near to the station in Bledlow, and the trains used to go past our front door. When we moved up to the Midlands, a Hickman's lorry came and shifted all our furniture. Joe Connaughton and Jim Bancroft were on the lorry we had, and funnily enough my Grandad once drove for that firm too. As a three-year-old I can vaguely remember my mother, father, my two sisters, Edie and Winnie, and me going up to Staffordshire. It seemed to take all day to get there, but then in those days the lorries only did about 20mph. We moved to the Midlands so that my mother could look after her Dad who had recently been widowed. We settled in Lapley, about twelve miles from Wolverhampton, and I did all my schooling there too. Dad worked for the Staffordshire Council for about 25s a week, and it was around this time that my interest in football first started. My Uncle used to take me to Molineux to see Wolverhampton Wanderers play and from then on they were to be my team. He would stick me down the front against the railings and then he would take me home after the game. When I was a little older, Mum used to put me and my sisters on the train at Wolverhampton station under the

care of the guard, and we would come back to Risborough for our summer holidays. When I finally left school, work was scarce but I managed to begin my engineering life at a small local company. They didn't have much work, so to try and earn some money I then got a job as an errand boy. But eventually the chance came to take up an apprenticeship and I did a five year course as a turner and that was to stand me in good stead for the rest of my working life.

His Dad actually moved back south around 1937 and bought a house in Berryfield Road, Princes Risborough, but Harold stayed in the Midlands for a few more years. On one of his trips back to Bucks though, Harold, who had by then married his Staffordshire-born wife, Ivy, bought a plot of land next to his Dad's house in Berryfield. Harold says, 'The plot was 80ft and I paid £2 10s 0d per foot!' The couple had every intention of moving south as soon as he could leave his engineering company. But his engineering skills were desperately wanted during the war years and his was a reserved occupation. Harold spent the war making vital parts for tanks. But the pull of the Chilterns did finally bring him back south again. Around 1948 he returned to live in Princes Risborough with his wife and young son, Brian, and their first house was in Station Road. It was a wooden building that used to be a fish and chip shop. Harold recalls:

After a while we had to take down this wooden structure as they didn't want it in Station Road. It was in sections and the builder was able to take it apart, move the sections to our plot of land in Berryfield Road and rebuild it there. Because it was classed as a temporary building, we had to obtain a permit every year to live there. In the end though, they wouldn't give us a permit any longer and we then built the bungalow where I still live today.

At the time Berryfield Road ended at his house:

There was a farm gate outside our front and the fields stretched all the way to Whiteleaf. They used to play football and cricket in those fields and I used to pick potatoes from there for Stan Woods and his brothers who owned the land. We were surrounded by fields in those days.

Harold was by then working for Broom & Wade in High Wycombe but in 1954 he was to find a new job at Molins in Saunderton. Anyone who knows Harold and his family will forever associate him with Molins, and the stories he tells of his life at the Tobacco Machinery factory would fill several of these books:

At Broom & Wade I was on just under £6 a week, but when I went to Molins I was on £10 a week and I thought I was a millionaire! Molins was a great firm to work for and we had some smashing lads working in the Light Machine shops. We had great fun and they were always playing practical jokes on each other. I remember one chap called Towers, who was a devil, always doing something. One day he managed to get hold of our labourer's broom and, taking a box of Swan Vesta, he carefully placed lots of the matches in amongst the bristles. When poor old Taffy, our labourer, next picked up his broom to sweep the shop, WHOOSH, the whole lot went up in flames!

Then there was the occasion, in my early days there, when my supervisor brought in a goose. He gave me a time card to cover my hours, just so I could spend all day plucking that

Harold Mitchell at the Back Lane Fête, back row, fourth from the right..

blooming bird for him. There were feathers and down everywhere, and I was supposed to be an engineer! Anyway, when I finally finished, he took it to our canteen where one of the dinner ladies then trussed it up ready for the oven. By the time my supervisor went home it was all ready to cook, all prepared on Molins time.

Harold was not averse to joining in some of the stunts the lads got up to. In fact he instigated many of them. He once bought himself a tandem and one Christmas, when on the nightshift, he took the bike into the factory in the back of his van. He had also borrowed a couple of Father Christmas outfits and when he arrived at the factory he unloaded his bike, changed into his outfit, collared his mate Pete Boland, who put the other suit on, and they then promptly set off on a tour of the factory on the tandem. They rode through the shops, past an unsuspecting night manager in his office, and down to the canteen, the Heavy Machine shop and all round the site. Two blokes coming out of the toilet nearly choked with shock as they saw two Father Christmases ride past on a tandem! The night manager never did find out what all the fuss was about as Harold and Pete changed back to their 'civvies' and carried on working as though nothing had happened. Harold remembers:

All was going well until I turned right on the bike and Pete thought I was going left and fell off! To see this roly-poly Father Christmas rolling around the light machine shop was one of the funniest sights ever and I still laugh when I think about it to this day.

Harold later made full use of that costume by appearing regularly as Father Christmas at Berryfield School and also for the Molins children's Christmas parties.

Harold did well at Molins and later became a chargehand in the Turning shop:

> The day they made me a chargehand, everyone waited for me as I appeared for the first time in my pristine white coat. They whooped and hollered and made such a racket to welcome their new 'boss'. Although actually, they were doing what came naturally to them all, they were taking the P!

Molins was only a small part of the life of this remarkable man. He had always loved football, was a player himself, a left half, in the Wolverhampton Amateur League, and then also played for Parkfield Rovers after he came to Risborough. He later became involved with his son's football team and helped run the Under-12s side:

> By the early 1950s the Berryfield estate was growing fast and because the houses were all being built by Wimpey, we called our lads' team Wimpic Wanderers. We used to play against several other sides in the town, like the Methodist Church team, but gradually these other teams all folded. However, our side was still going strong and in the end, as the boys grew older, a few of us adults got together to form Risborough Tenants Football Club, mainly because most of the lads came from Risborough. We originally played on the field past Chev's factory down the Longwick Road. I remember one game when we played Hazells in a cup match in Aylesbury. They beat us 24-0! At Longwick Road we changed in the Scout hut and then walked down the road to play the games. When we had the chance to obtain the site at the end of Salisbury Close, we moved up to there. They were laying some water mains pipes somewhere around

Two Santas on a tandem.

the town, and all the loose earth was being dumped at that Salisbury Close site. At the end of the day we were able to arrange for the earth to be levelled off and made suitable for football. The number of stones was horrendous and over many weekends the players, friends and families went across that pitch picking up all the stones. It was ages before it was cleared.

That was only the start, as Harold continued not only to prepare the ground for matches, but also to lead many of the fundraising drives to raise money for the club. One of the things he did was to collect waste paper. He gathered all the waste paper from Molins and other places, loaded it onto his van, and took it to a paper merchant, where he was able to sell it and hand the money over to help keep the club going. And all the railings around the ground that you see today were also put there by the work of Harold Mitchell and his friend, Tom Earle:

We got all the piping from Molins ['Offcuts,' he said with a smile!], managed to get someone to dig the holes for us, mixed the cement and then carefully put the railings in. We had to work quickly though, before the cement set. It was tough work, but they are still there to this day, so we must have done a good job.

If all this work for the football team wasn't enough, there was still his allotment to keep up:

When my Dad came back to Risborough he had an allotment and he actually opened a small shop in the garage of his house. He would go backwards and forwards to his allotment picking all the fresh vegetables to sell at his shop. Then later, when I had an allotment, I did the same for him. I used to grow a bit of everything on that allotment down the Longwick Road, and I remember taking my wheelbarrow in the back of my van and filling it to the brim with runner beans! After Dad died, I had a little stall at the end of my drive and continued to sell fresh fruit and vegetables for a long time. At one time, I had ten allotments.

Many of the people we interviewed have fond memories of that shop of Mr Mitchell Senior. Co-author Angela Payne recalls:

We used to love going in to Mr Mitchell's shop, as he also used to sell sweets for the children. When we were at the Top School we had to walk down to the Berryfield Road School to have our cookery and rural science lessons. On the way we would always pop into the shop for some sweets. Mr Mitchell was always sat there in his chair; we often wondered if he ever moved from the shop. He looked very smart and had a suit on, and he was always cheerful and eager to please us children.

Harold, meanwhile, found another thing to do with his time. He became a roadie for The Dave Peterson Five band:

I don't quite remember how I got involved with them, although a couple of the lads worked at Molins. They were looking for somebody to take them to their gigs and I happened to say one day that I would do it. By the time the group finished I was even taking the bookings for them. We did cover some miles, mostly local places, and when we were all crammed in my van with all their gear, there wasn't a lot of room. I remember one night gig we did at a big house near Henley. We left in daylight and came home in daylight. They had this big heated swimming pool and after our gig was over, we all took our clothes off and dived in for a swim. It was lovely. Old Sheik [Dave Farris], the drummer with the band, had a big moustache and when he was in that pool he looked just like a walrus!

Rumour still has it that it was a session of skinny-dipping, but Harold denies this and swears he had some trunks on. On another night, whilst the boys played their gig, Harold was sat in his van. Suddenly two blokes walked past carrying a large armchair. He went into the building and told one of the organisers in there. It turned out that they were actually stealing the chair and the owners ended up chasing after them to get it back. 'We had so much fun with that band,' says Harold, 'things were always happening to us, but I wouldn't have missed the experience for anything.'

Harold loved his old vans and one Bedford Dormobile was a particularly familiar sight around Risborough. Not only did he ferry the band to their gigs, but he also used it to take the footballers to away games. On one very cold day he got the van out of his garage, picked up all the lads and set off for the game. When they reached Amersham, the van suddenly seized up and came to a halt with steam and smoke billowing out of the engine. What Harold had forgotten was that because of the severity of the frost the night before he had put an old coat over the engine to protect it. He had driven all the way to Amersham with the coat still there!

Not only were there the van and the tandem, there was also another form of transport Harold had a passion for, and that was motorbikes:

> My first bike was a Long Stroke Sunbeam and then I had a Calthorpe, and also a 1937 Rudge Special. I think it must have been the engineer in me that appreciated all the clever work that went into building them. I remember, years later, getting a good price for those old bikes as they eventually became real collector's items.

There was hardly a trader in the town that Harold didn't help out with his van over the years. He was very friendly with the Woods farming family, and he often helped out the four brothers, Rupert, Stan, Ron and Reg:

> If Reg was ill, I used to do his milk round for him before I went to work. I remember once calling on Mr Percival of Adcock & Percival at his home at the end of the Avenue. It was a good job I had my gloves on that day, because his dog went for me and ripped my glove clean off. I had a right go at Mr Percival and I said that if the dog did it again I would whack it with a milk bottle! I often nipped down to the station to pick things up and funnily enough, I used to get my haircut done in the larger signal box. My brother-in-law was a driver for Witcher's Taxis and he used to take me over to Dave Pinfold, one of the signalmen, to get my hair cut.

Ivy Mitchell on her husband's Rudge motorcycle.

Another memory he has of the railway highlights one of the old lines out of Risborough Station, long since gone. When his daughter, Linda, was born in the Watlington Hospital, Harold pedalled down to the station on his bike, loaded it on the train and travelled to Watlington Station. He got off there and then rode to the hospital to see his wife and new daughter, before making the reverse journey back home again.

We called this chapter 'It's Been a Busy Life', and it was not unusual for Harold's day to be something like this: do Woods's milk round, go to work, nip up to Tenants and mark the pitch and put the nets up, go down to the allotments and pick the vegetables for the shop and for dinner, take the footballers to their game, bring them home and pick up the band and take them to their gig, bring them home, say hello to Ivy, have a tinker with the motorbikes, wrap a coat around the van engine and go to bed for a couple of hours sleep before it starts all over again!

Harold Mitchell is one of Princes Risborough's most enduring and amazing characters, who has enjoyed a long and eventful life. He could certainly talk for England! So we will let him have the last word or two:

Some of the folks I've met I could tell you a tale about, like Frank Stables who used to work nights with me at Molins. He was a bit religious and he would start singing hymns on the night shift, and in the end we would all be singing along with him! Then there was Tom Bennett who always had a pipe on, even when he ran the line for us at football. Then there was Daisy Saw, what a character she was! She used to arrange coach trips to the coast that we all went on. There was the 'Midnight Baker' at the top of the High Street near the White Lion pub, Chester his name was, and he used to bake all day and deliver late into the night. Old George Jacobs, he was another, he once built a small steam engine that he used to ride round the High Street on. Then there was Bookie, he chased me once and we had an argument about speeding, which I wasn't. He never booked me that day as it happens. Then there was Oscar Wheatley, who had very large ears and poked everyone with his walking stick. As he went in Robin Ball's shop, Robin would say, 'Here comes Oscar, coming in to land!' The list is endless and the memory of all these people will stay with me forever.

Molins staff gather in the Stores for a retirement presentation.

Chapter Sixteen

Thanks for the Memories

We have spoken to many people over the past year, and they all have their own vivid memories of living and working in Princes Risborough during the past seventy years and seeing the changes in the town. Here is a small selection from the memories of some of those Risborough folk.

Nigel Fountain – Once Here, Never Forgotten

When young Nigel Fountain came to live in Kingsmead, Monks Risborough, during the Second World War years, it was to leave a lasting imprint on his mind about Princes Risborough. Nigel's father worked for a firm called Belling & Lee, who were based in Enfield, where his family originally came from, but after the war broke out, the company moved out to the country and set up in part of the Cheverton & Laidler factory in Church Square. Nigel recalls:

Towards the end of the war Belling & Lee also built some temporary prefab-type buildings on the land between what is now Manor Park Avenue and Stratton Road. They were a firm who made numerous radar and other electronic components, and also VHF aerials for use in aircraft. When the firm moved out of Enfield to set up in Risborough, we set up home at No. 8 Kingsmead with my father, Leslie, mother, Vera, my Grandmother, Eva Fountain, and her sister, Mabel White, in Monks Risborough and stayed here for the duration of the war. I have fond memories of living in Monks Risborough and going to school there and making the daily walk up Mill Lane. I was in Mrs Fowler's class at Monks Risborough School, but cannot remember very much now about my time there. I do remember learning to write letters of the alphabet in lines drawn on paper or the blackboard, ensuring that the tails of the letters went above and below these lines. A regular game in the playground was 'What's the time, Mr Wolf?', but we frequently hung over the railings to watch Army vehicles trundle past the school in convoy, with tanks, etc. I also used to walk home for lunch every day, so walking four lots of three-quarters of a mile a day was no problem. I remember there was a girl's boarding school near the War Memorial in Mill Lane and, I think, a POW camp further on before the bungalows. All those memories came flooding back last year when I visited an exhibition put on at the school, showing 150 years of its existence.

Nigel can still recall his childhood with great affection and, as he says, a bicycle was a necessity for getting around in those days:

As a family we would cycle miles around the area, and we also spent many hours catching butterflies, a very common sight in the countryside back then. It is an illegal practice now, but I still have some of the butterflies I collected when I lived in Monks, in a couple of boxes in my loft. When we were at home we would play in the road and the adjoining fields, or sometimes on the railway line near Monks Risborough and Whiteleaf Halt, as it was known then. The occasional steam trains on the line could always be heard coming. I actually used to go to Princes Risborough station frequently to watch the trains, where the single track to Aylesbury required the engine driver to carry a hoop-shaped piece of metal to confirm he had the right of way on the track. There was also a single-carriage diesel train, which went to Watlington, quite a thrill to ride on in those times. We occasionally went to London by train, Paddington rather than Marylebone I am sure in those days, via High Wycombe and Gerrards Cross. One thing I do remember is coming home later in the evening from Paddington when there was always one express train, which operated what they called a 'slip coach'. As we approached the station the last carriage would be detached from the moving train, around Saunderton I think, and all passengers for Princes Risborough had to be in that carriage. After it had rolled on to become stationary, a local engine would pick up the carriage and take it into the station, whilst the express itself went north, without stopping at Risborough. We would then continue our journey home to Monks Risborough on the single track Aylesbury line.

It was hard to believe that a war was on at times, but of course there were often stark reminders. Nigel continues:

I recall hearing the sirens going off at the beginning and end of an air raid, a terrifying sound to me. We occasionally heard a doodlebug [V1 or V2 rocket] going overhead, and I remember once we heard the engine cut out on one of them, but I was never sure where it fell. My father played snooker at the Princes Risborough Institute during the war and I sometimes used to go and watch him play, sitting on the raised seating by the window. That was a very dark and dreary room. A frequent Sunday afternoon outing was to the local library, which was in Whiteleaf. This was in an old wooden building that only opened on a Sunday afternoon. Then we would sometimes go up to the top of the cross and I remember both my parents played golf at the Whiteleaf Golf Course, where later, in 1952, I played my first ever game of golf.

Two other wartime memories I have was of my Grandmother serving at a tearooms in the Market Square and of both my parents having all their teeth removed at the dentist near the George & Dragon, common practice in those days! When the war ended there were street parties in Risborough to celebrate, and we had one at Kingsmead for the twenty or so children that lived there at the time. And one of my last memories before we moved was of

Winston Churchill making a speech from his open-top car in the Market Square in July 1945 during the election campaign.

Later that same month Nigel and his family moved back to Enfield, but it was not to be his last connection with Princes Risborough:

My Grandmother and my Aunt moved to No. 5 Berryfield Road after we moved, and they were to stay there until 1952. At the time, Berryfield only had around eight houses and the road came to an abrupt end at the fields beyond the last house. My Grandmother and Aunt were the daughters of a Baptist minister and both, as far as I recall, attended the Baptist Chapel in Risborough throughout their time in the town. Around 1950 my Grandmother's sister-in-law, Rose Anderson (née Fountain), came from the Shetland Isles with her husband, the Reverend Robert Anderson, to live in No. 5 Park Street. Apparently he was a minister in the Shetlands. He died in Risborough in 1954, aged seventy-five, and is buried in the Baptist Chapel cemetery. His wife Rose died in 1962, in Hampstead aged ninety-seven, and is buried with him.

So Nigel Fountain has a lot of memories of Princes Risborough from a relatively short period of time. He has never forgotten his days here, and his final thoughts were:

I remember vividly spending several Christmases at my Grandmother's house and I grew to know Princes Risborough very well over the years. I was a keen photographer in my youth

Nigel Fountain's Great Aunt and Grandmother at their Berryfield home.

and took several pictures around the town, developing them myself. It always brings back fond memories for me when I look at them.

Some of those pictures have been used in this book and we are grateful to Nigel for allowing their use.

Gordon Todd – Learning a Trade

Gordon Todd was born in Ilmer and lived in Kimblewick for four years, starting school at Kimble before his family moved to Cannon Place in Princes Risborough in 1936. When he left school in 1941, he went to work in the aircraft factory near the station in the building that is now Hypnos. Furniture was built there both before and after the war, but during the war, the factory was taken over so that they could make training aircraft for the RAF and Navy. The Miles Master and then later, the Miles Martinet, was built in sections at the factory. When the sections were finished they would be shipped off to Woodley, near Reading, to be assembled and the aircraft completed. The planes were primarily used for pulling targets so that pilots could be trained in the art of warfare.

Gordon Todd spent a year helping out in all the shops on the factory floor, using his skills as a carpenter on the all-wood-built aeroplane. Later he moved on to help put the skins around the centre portion of the fuselage. He remembers the night the unexploded bomb fell in Clifford Road:

> I was working at the factory at the time, and so was my Dad, Walter Todd, who was a security policeman and ARP warden there. He had been wounded in the First World War having had part of his arm shot away serving with the Royal Artillery. Dad worked nights at the factory and on that particular night, I was at home in Cannon Place with my Mum, Louisa. We heard the air-raid alarm go off and then we suddenly heard the sound of the bombs screeching down. Dad had built us a shelter in the garden but there was no time to get there, and Mum and me just dived under the table for cover. But strangely there was no explosion and of course, the next day we discovered the news about the unexploded bomb in Clifford Road. I believe there was actually more than one, but Risborough was lucky that night, that's for sure.

When the war was coming to an end, Gordon joined the Army, the 1st Battalion Ox & Bucks Infantry Regiment, and in fact was sent to Berlin after his many weeks of training:

> I was in Berlin for Christmas 1945, and it was an experience to see just what our bombers had done to the German city. In the end I spent three and a half years in the Army before coming back to Risborough in 1948 and then finding a job as a maintenance worker with the railway. I worked with several Polish lads at the time, and we were responsible for all the repairs on the stations from Gerrards Cross right up to Ardley, plus all the branch lines to Oxford and Aylesbury. We basically repaired anything that was broken; windows, doors, lights and even the farm gates and stiles alongside the track. I was also another who had his hair cut by Dave Pinfold in the North Signal Box at Risborough Station!

In 1949, Gordon married Ruby Read in St Mary's Church, and for three years they lived in rented rooms in Park Street, before having the chance to move into the house in Berryfield Road where Gordon still lives. Ruby was originally from Waddesdon, but she later became a familiar face in the Risborough shops as she worked for Padley's the chemist for many years. Gordon recalls:

> We had some lovely years together, and we were blessed with two children, Sally and Derek. We both worked hard but we had fun too. I was a keen footballer and I played in goal for Princes Risborough before it later became Risborough Town FC. We won the league and the cup one year. Our pitch used to be in Berryfield Road, with one goal almost level with where my garden is now, and the other goal down towards the town. Remember, there was no estate at the back of Berryfield in those days, and it was only later that the team started to use the Windsor Playing Fields at Horsenden. One local derby I always remembered playing in was against a team called Parkfield Rovers, who played where the Avenue is now. I was a bit frail for a goalkeeper but I played behind some great players, especially Alfie White, who was one of the best centre halves I ever saw.

When we began talking with Gordon about the police in the town, he recalled a couple of incidents that almost gave him a record!

> Years ago, there was a group of us that went to the old Carlton Cinema one summer's evening. When we came out we were larking about and in those days, more of the shopkeepers used to have blinds that they would pull out to shield the shops from the sun. Anyway, we decided that we would all climb up onto one of these blinds and it collapsed!

Gordon Todd, goalkeeper for Parkfield Rovers.

Unfortunately, someone saw us and reported us to the police, and we had to attend the court at the Literary Institute a few days later and we were each fined five bob! On another day, and this shows you how antiquated the laws were in the 1950s, Ruby and me, and a few friends, Danny Richer and Dick Hill and their wives, made our usual Sunday visit to the Nags Head pub in Monks Risborough. They used to have a small separate room in the back, with a lovely cosy fire and a bar billiards table. Now, you couldn't play bar billiards on a Sunday back then, but the landlord said that it would be alright on this occasion if we locked the door. This we did, but soon afterwards there came a knock on the door. The landlady quickly realised what was happening and smuggled our wives out of the room. When we opened the door there was the local bobby, Bernard Loosley. And he nabbed us for playing bar billiards on a Sunday! Another five bob fine each, although this time settled out of court! Ironically, my mate, Dick Hill, later went on to achieve quite a high rank as a police officer himself.

Gordon's working career as a carpenter continued well past his retirement age, and having worked for a few local firms, including Chev's for a couple of years, he eventually found himself at Leo Laboratories. When he was due to retire at sixty-five, they asked if he would stay on for a while. He did and carried on part-time until he was seventy. Coupled with his love of fishing, he became a very familiar Risborough character. 'The town has changed a lot since I moved here in 1936 but I've had a happy time and met up with some great friends and characters who have lived here.' We asked him finally if he particularly remembered any of those characters. He said, 'One I remember very well was Dicky Jacobs, a blacksmith in Back Lane. Liked his drink did Dicky!'

Gordon remembers how different it was living in Berryfield Road before the rest of that estate was built. The sight of lapwings and skylarks out of their back window has long gone, sadly. But he and Ruby had fifty-four happy years together before her death, and as Gordon says, 'The day she died was the worst day of my life.'

Marion Makepeace – Coming to Risborough, An Outsider's Experience

When Marion Smith and her family moved from Deptford, in London, to Princes Risborough in 1953, it was because her Dad, George, would be able to transfer to the new factory that had been built at Saunderton, called Molins. The family was the first of many that made this move from the city. Marion remembers:

Mr Whittaker, the personnel manager, brought us from Deptford by car and first took us for a tour of the factory. One of the things I remember most about that was being shown inside the men's toilet. That was embarrassing for an eight-year-old girl! Later he took us on to have our first look at Princes Risborough, and as we drove through the town I was struck by what a bustling little place it was. When we first came to live here, we lived in a house called 'Greensleeves' on the Longwick Road. The house still has that name, but whereas the Police Station is now next door, in those days it was all woods and trees and a great place to play.

The family were pioneers in some respects but it was a daunting time for them, trying to integrate with the local people. Marion continues:

> School in Deptford was Lucas Vale, a three-storey modern building, and we were assured that I would have a place at Bell Street School if we moved to Risborough. The promise wasn't kept and I found myself in the small Church School, which consisted of three small rooms and two small blocks of outside toilets. As I recall, your age dictated which room your class was in and it was with relief when the winter came that my class could have the middle room. The reason being it was the only room with a fire in! The different teaching methods from one school to the other, plus the fact I had a strong London accent and didn't understand a lot of what was being said, made life quite difficult. Contracting childhood illnesses like scarlet fever, and being clouted a few times by some of my classmates because I was 'different', didn't help either, and it made me seek drastic action. This took the form of refusing to go to school. Unfortunately my Dad had other ideas and carried me over his shoulder from our Longwick Road house to the school! But gradually, especially after the Molins estate was built at Fairway, we began to make friends, initially amongst the fellow Londoners, and then eventually we won the Risborough folk over and we all settled.

It was fair to say that there was some resentment from the locals towards the Londoners who had come out of the capital to take jobs at the Molins factory. But Molins was eventually to be a golden nugget for Princes Risborough's economy and by the time the 1960s and 1970s came round, it was *the* place to work in the area.

It was not all bad memories for Marion in those early days and she still had her family:

> My Dad was a keen pianist and often treated us all to a sing-song. I remember that when we lived in Longwick Road we often saw the nuns file past our front. They would be in two columns and everyone would stop and stare as they walked down the road. One day my Dad saw them going past, opened the windows, and immediately played 'Walking Beside You' on the piano, much to Mum's embarrassment.

As the years passed and Marion began to join in with the local youth clubs and other local events, the inevitable happened. She met a local boy, Colyn 'Nibbo' Makepeace at the Stewart Hall in Kimble, and they immediately hit it off. Even at that time though, Marion's family were still coming to terms with country life:

> My Mum and Dad used to get really cross if a herd of cows were being herded along the road holding them up, and dropping all sorts of 'waste material' onto the road. Nibbo used to wind me up by saying that it was Risborough's last protest against the Molins crowd!

After a while Marion and Nibbo went their separate ways, but eventually they were to get together again, and in 1973 they married. By now Nibbo was a successful plumber in the town and Marion decided to venture into a business herself. Risborough had a small market on the car park of the old Buckingham Arms pub in the early 1980s, and Marion began to sell baby and children's clothes. She recalls:

It was great fun doing that market, but hard work too, some cold days my hands were almost too frozen to pitch my stall! I had to wear about ten layers of clothes some days! But having the stall did give me the chance to really get to know some of the people of the town, and for them to get to know me too. I used to do the market stall on my own and I also did the Amersham market and the Chesham market. I did try Aylesbury market for a short while but that was too difficult on my own, ferrying the stock backwards and forwards. But that market experience led directly to me opening my first shop, in Bell Street in 1985. That was a daunting thing to do and the high shop rent and business rates added to the extra pressure. But those early years couldn't have gone better as we were really busy and had lots of regular customers. It was indicative of Risborough's busy shops at the time.

Later Marion expanded her business and opened a second shop in the premises next to the Baptist Chapel entrance, Lydia Carter's old shop:

We kept the first shop, and the name 'Tops & Bottoms', for about a year before merging everything into one, and by this time we were selling male and female fashions as well as children's wear. Lydia Carter's beauty salon was actually run by Eve Whitehead, and she kept on a part of the business in the back of our shop, for one or two of her beauty treatments. We became good friends and I remember her and her husband, Wilf, inviting us for drinks

Buckingham Arms market.

Marian Makepeace's shop Tops & Bottoms.

on a Saturday evening after a week's work, in their flat above the shop. Nibbo used to join us and we would enjoy the relaxation. However, by the time we went home we were a little bit merry, to say the least, and a lot of my Sundays were spent recovering!

Marion had several people working with her through these years. Amongst them were Carol Evans and Pauline Clay, and at times they had some great fun:

It was a pleasure running that business, although we did have one or two incidents over the years. I remember being at home once when Carol rang me from the shop. Typically I was in the bath at the time! Anyway she rang to ask if I could come straight to the shop, as there was man in there who was flashing! I only had a towel wrapped round me at the time, but quickly threw on a coat, not bothering with underwear, and rushed to the shop. By the time I got there, the man was fully dressed and had more clothes on than I did!

In the 1990s it became more and more difficult to run a retail business in Princes Risborough. Trade was down throughout the town and other bigger retail outlets were dominating the clothes market. To Marion's lasting regret she reluctantly decided to close the shop in 1994:

It was increasingly hard to make any money in the business and with rents and business rates going up and up, then sadly it doesn't encourage small businesses to continue. This is seen now in Princes Risborough in the number of empty shops there are. I think it will get worse before it gets better.

Marion has now worked for many years at Mencap, and although she finds the work rewarding, she still misses the people coming in to her shop and the fun she had during those days. She wouldn't have missed it for the world.

Jean Stevens (née Munday) – Life and Top School Revisited

Jean Munday was born in her Aunt's house in Wycombe Road and her Mother, Connie, was also born in Princes Risborough, at Poppy Road. Her grandparents lived in Parkfield, so all in all Jean's family were steeped in Risborough traditions.

After leaving school, Connie worked as an upholstery machinist at the Goodearl's furniture factory and during the war she spent her time sewing silk parachute covers. Jean's father, Ed, had his family roots in Ewelme, Oxfordshire. Both Connie and Ed were greatly affected by events during the war. Ed was a gunner with the First Airlanding Light Regiment, Royal Artillery, and saw some tough fighting at Arnhem, and Connie lost her brother, Freddie, who was killed in Italy in 1943, aged just twenty. However, after the war Ed met Connie through a quirk of fate when his cousin Pat, who also worked with Connie at the factory, introduced them. The couple courted, and eventually they were married at St Mary's Church in 1947. Ironically, after their wedding, Ed also worked in Goodearl's furniture factory. His job was as a stoker in the boiler room. Jean remembers, 'Dad used to have a visit from the local bobby on cold days, primarily so that the PC could get warm!'

Like everyone else in this book, Jean has fond memories of shopping in the town and especially of Adcock & Percival's shop, but one memory she had of the shop was one that others had not mentioned. Jean recalls:

I loved going in there, with the grocery store one side and the newspapers, sweets and toys on the other. The coffee beans roasting was an unforgettable smell, and Adcocks was *the* place for all the Risborough gossip, but one thing they had in the window always caught my eye. They used to post a black-edged sign highlighting funeral announcements. Shopping seemed easier and quicker in those days and I use to love choosing my Christmas presents with Mum after school, ticking present ideas off my list, perhaps buying bath cubes or talc from Padley's for my Granny, for instance.

In the early 1950s the people of the town saw various groceries gradually coming off ration. Just like today the rising prices were a major talking point amongst the shoppers. It often took a while to get home after a shopping trip and Jean remembers on many occasions walking up the street and seeing her Mum stop to talk to friends about things like salt coming off ration and going up a penny! Everyone seemed outraged.

School was not something Jean has too many fond memories of, although she does remember being one of the first children to go abroad on a school trip. School trips abroad are now common practice but in the late 1950s and early 1960s it was a new idea, and money was tight, but Jean's parents scrimped and saved so that Jean could go on a trip to Paris. She also remembers the children that had come down from London to live in Risborough, and helping them to integrate into the local school. She enjoyed helping at

Children's party at Goodearl's factory.

the youth club at St Mary's Church Hall in Church Lane and also remembers going to dances and discos at both the Walsingham Hall and the Whitecross Hall. She eventually stayed on at school until she was sixteen and was determined to try and find a career. Jean continues:

> There was not very much by way of careers advice for schoolchildren in my day, but I really had ambitions to find myself a worthwhile career, such as an author or journalist. In the end I had to lower my sights a little, although I was able to embark on a two-year secretarial course. It gave me the chance to build on my typing and shorthand skills that I had learned at the age of thirteen in Mrs Ede's home school classes next to the Bird in Hand in Station Road. I always enjoyed learning and many years later I achieved several qualifications, including undergraduate and graduate degrees, inspired by the Julie Walters film *Educating Rita*!

Growing up in the 1960s was an exciting time for teenagers and Jean was one of many who recorded the top-ten records from the radio programme *Pick of the Pops*. She also remembers buying records in Purcell's record shop in Duke Street:

> Like many other girls I wanted to marry Paul McCartney, but was actually a Stones fan more than The Beatles. And for a while I also liked Lonnie Donegan and bought quite a few of my record collection in Purcells. I was also a Saturday girl at Walker's Stores, remember going to pictures at the Carlton Cinema, where my Uncle was a projectionist, and I also recall going to film shows that they put on occasionally in the British Legion. I went to Sunday school at

the Baptist Chapel and was thrilled to win a prize or two, usually a book for my attendance record there. And I also loved the times that I spent having a picnic on the hills around the West Wycombe Mausoleum. The other highlight each year was the visit to Risborough of the fair. They were really good in those days and we would hang around the dodgems, chatting to the boys. The night would be completed with a bag of chips on the way home.

Sadly, Jean's parents both died within a few days of each other at the end of 2008, but they never lost their love of living in the town, where they were known and liked by many people.

In 1995, Jean was the instigator of a reunion at the Top School for the 'Class of '65' and it was a resounding success. People came from as far afield as Wales, Peterborough and the Cotswolds to attend the event, which was combined with a reunion for the 'Class of '70'. There were also letters from ex-pupils from the USA and Australia offering their support for the evening, in spirit at least. It took a great deal of work to organise and Jean was helped by her husband, Chris, but all the effort was worthwhile as people met up again some thirty years after they left school. Several of the teachers came to the event with Lou Emmett, Jean and Roger Fincher, Bernard and Auriole Hodge, and Alan Goodwright all in attendance. It was also the chance for former pupils such as Bob Goodchild, John Angood, Pat Dennis (née Small), Brenda Stockbridge (née Pinnells), Colin Steptoe, Melvyn Johnson and many others to see who had aged the most in thirty years, and who had prospered most! Jean sums up what that evening meant, 'One of our teachers said we were the last of a special group of children, born into fairly tough times as far as money was concerned, but generally having respect for each other, our parents and the teachers.'

Top School reunion of the classes of 1965 to 1970.

Final Thoughts

It is now seventy years since the outbreak of the Second World War and the changes seen in the country over that period of time are many and varied. Princes Risborough has a unique story to tell, and in the pages of this book, we hope we have captured a flavour of how it has evolved.

Just as England has always been a country built around the people who live there, the same can certainly be said about the town of Princes Risborough.

Mike and Angela Payne
October 2009

A Personal Memory by Janet Preston

Risborough

What I remember about this town
Set under the cross, hills all around.
Bluebell woods and primrose banks
I look to my childhood with heartfelt thanks.

In winter should we get some snow
To the chalk pits, off we'd go,
Homemade sledges, which Dad had invented,
Mine fell to bits as it first descended.

Back to the drawing board, Father went,
With hammer and nails which were quickly spent.
Model two soon appeared, Dad was never defeated,
But the thing was too heavy, after he had completed.
(He threw in the towel after that)

At six o'clock on the first of May
Fiddles playing we would stay
To country dance around the square
Not many of us would be there.

Summer saw Monks Risborough show
Held where the Paddocks resides now
The Legion also held a fête
Residents never missed that date

Down the High Street, twice a day
Wood's cows would wend their way
Mr East with his cart and horse
Delivered our coal with extras of course
(The roses and rhubarb loved it)

Do you remember Adcock & Percivals
Next to the butcher's, with toys just so magical
The smell of coffee would waft up and down
I'd stand at the window, while the drum went round

I love this place
It's all I've known
I've travelled the world
But so glad to get **home.**

Other titles published by The History Press

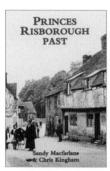

Princes Risborough Past
SANDY MACFARLANE & CHRIS KINGHAM

Princes Risborough has grown in the past fifty years from a quiet agricultural market village into a busy and predominantly commuter town. The change has been achieved sympathetically by balanced growth around the old heart of the town whereby its impact on this outstandingly beautiful area has been minimised. Profusely illustrated by pictures and documents it is a very readable book. It has been a labour of love for its authors who have both spent many years putting together this splendid picture of the past of this charming Buckinghamshire town.

978 1 8607 7047 0

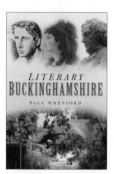

Literary Buckinghamshire
PAUL WREYFORD

Poet John Betjemen was not the only scribe 'beckoned out to lanes in beechy Bucks'. Many of the country's most famous writers shared his fondness for the county and sought solace within its boundaries. John Milton came here to escape the plague in London; Enid Blyton fled the capital's increasing development, while D.H. Lawrence and his German wife took refuge on the outbreak of the First World War.

978 0 7509 4959 0

No Finer Courage: A Village in the Great War
MICHAEL SENIOR

History tells us that no community in Britain escaped the carnage of the First World War. Up and down the country, war memorials bear silent testimony to the men who went away to fight and never returned. The Lee – a village in Buckinghamshire – was certainly no different. Michael Senior's compelling narrative interweaves everyday village life and events on the Western Front, drawing on a wide range of unpublished letters, diaries, memoirs and newspapers.

978 0 7509 3666 8

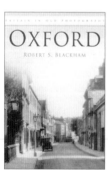

Oxford In Old Photographs
ROBERT S. BLACKHAM

This fascinating selection of 180 archive postcards and maps takes the reader on a nostalgic journey around historic Oxford, showcasing some of the finest buildings and streets in this English university city. The collection conjures a forgotten world of trams, horse-drawn buses, colleges, and the people connected with them though time. The book will stir nostalgic memories for some, and presents a unique view of the past for others, offering a glimpse of the city before the age of mass motor car ownership.

978 0 7524 5128 2

Visit our website and discover thousands of other History Press books.

www.thehistorypress.co.uk